SCIENCE

A SCHOLASTIC
KID'S
Encyclopedia

SCIENCE

David Rubel

An Agincourt Press Book

SCHOLASTIC
REFERENCE

NEW YORK · LONDON · TORONTO · AUCKLAND · SYDNEY

For Ben and Ella

AN AGINCOURT PRESS BOOK
President: David Rubel
Art Director: Tilman Reitzle
Editor: Sarah B. Weir

CONTRIBUTING EDITORS: Katherine Kirkpatrick, Julia Banks Rubel, Russell Shorto

COPY EDITOR: Ron Boudreau

DESIGN: Michael Hortens, Tilman Reitzle

PHOTO RESEARCH: Khara Nemitz, Kamau High, Diane F. Boudrez

We would especially like to thank Gary Brockman, Theron Cole, Breck P. Kent, and Kelly Wood of Nasco for their appreciable and appreciated contributions to this project.

PHOTO CREDITS appear on page 191.

Library of Congress Cataloging-in-Publication Data

Rubel, David.
Science/David Rubel.
p. cm. — (Scholastic kid's encyclopedia)
Includes index.
ISBN 0-590-49367-1
1. Science—Encyclopedias, Juvenile. [1. Science—Encyclopedias.] I. Title. II. Series.
Q121.R83 1995
500—dc20   94-46529
                                  CIP
                                  AC

12 11 10 9 8 7 6 5 4 3 2 1   5 6 7 8/9

Printed in the U.S.A.
First printing, October 1995

How to Use This Book

Topic

EACH TOPIC BEGINS WITH A SHORT DEFINITION.

Elmo shows you how the information relates to a child your age.

Important scientific topics from Adaptation to Wind are arranged in alphabetical order.

The topics are divided among five branches of science. Each branch is coded by color so that you can see how the topics are related.

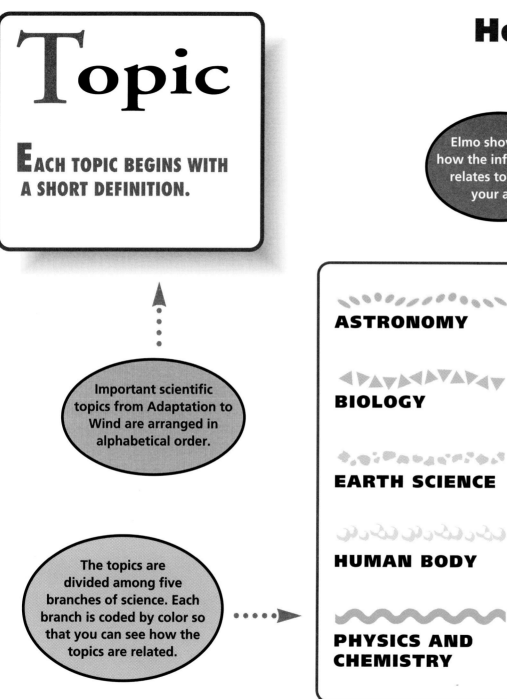

ASTRONOMY

BIOLOGY

EARTH SCIENCE

HUMAN BODY

PHYSICS AND CHEMISTRY

TABLE OF CONTENTS
The topics are listed in the table of contents. They are grouped according to the branch of science to which they belong. There is one page in the table of contents for each branch of science. The easiest topics to understand are marked with a • .

INDEX
You can use the index at the back of the book to look up specific subjects, such as dinosaurs or space flight, that may occur in more than one topic.

GLOSSARY
You can look up difficult words and scientific terms in the glossary at the back of the book.

LOOK UP: This space lists topics that explain or relate to the one you are reading.

Table of Contents

6

ASTRONOMY

BIOLOGY

EARTH SCIENCE

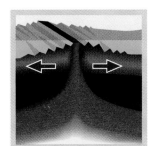

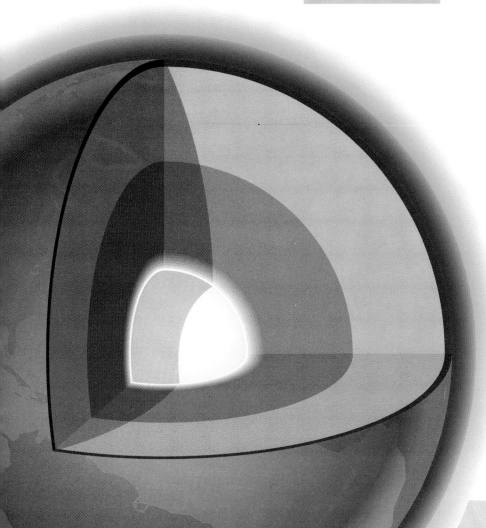

HUMAN BODY

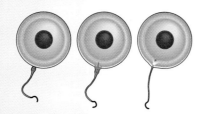

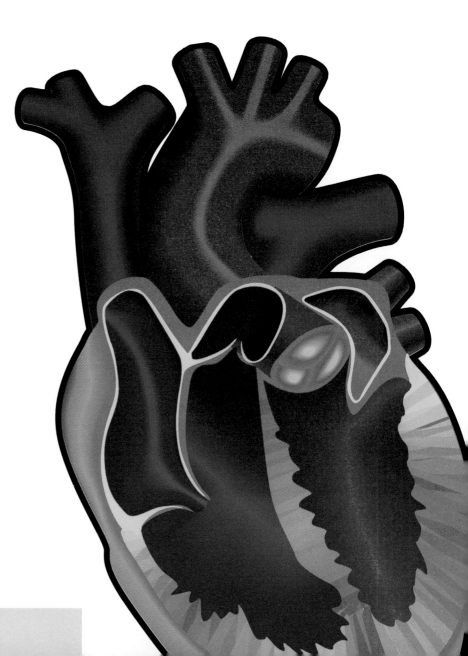

PHYSICS AND CHEMISTRY

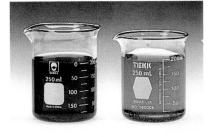

Adaptation

ADAPTATIONS ARE CHANGES THAT OCCUR IN LIVING THINGS. THEY CAN HELP ORGANISMS SURVIVE IN CHANGING ENVIRONMENTS.

ECOSYSTEMS ARE communities made up of living things, such as plants and animals, and the nonliving things that affect them.

Ecosystems contain habitats, or places where plants and animals live. In a forest, for example, trees are the most common habitat.

NICHE
Within an ecosystem, different species take advantage of different sources of food and shelter. Niches are slots in an ecosystem in which different species find food and shelter.

For example, although birds and mosses share the same habitat, they do not share the same niche. Birds live in the upper branches of trees, while mosses grow near the ground. Also, birds eat seeds, while mosses produce their own food.

In general, species adapt to fit a particular niche. For example, gerbils that live in the desert have claws so that they can dig burrows and escape the sun. Farther north, polar bears have heavy fur coats to help them survive the chilly Arctic winters.

The bottom of the ocean, where the DEEP-SEA ANGLERFISH lives, is dark. The anglerfish survives there by making its own light. At the tip of the "fishing pole" between its eyes is a shining light, which it uses to attract prey.

AVOIDING COMPETITION
In some niches, there are few competitors for food and shelter. For example, the dung fly flourishes in its niche because few animals compete with it for manure, which is plentiful.

Charles Darwin found that the Galápagos finches he studied had adapted in order

When reptiles first evolved from amphibians, they found many empty niches on land. Later, as these niches became more crowded, reptiles with wings appeared. These PTEROSAURS were the first animals to adapt to a previously empty niche—the sky.

to avoid competition. Some of these birds had large, powerful beaks, which they used to crack open the seeds they ate. Others had long, pointed beaks, which they used to dig out insects. In this way, evolutionary changes encouraged Galápagos finches to fill two types of niches: seed-eating niches and insect-eating niches.

ENVIRONMENTAL CHANGE

Some adaptations take millions of years. Others happen quickly. During the nineteenth century, when smoke began to pollute English industrial towns, soot carried by the smoke turned the bark of white trees gray. This environmental change affected the peppered moth, which lived in those trees.

The mostly white moths, which had been able to camouflage themselves, now stood out against the gray bark, making them easy prey for their enemies. Only the darker moths could hide.

Because of this advantage, the darker moths survived to pass on their genes, while the lighter moths were eaten.

Within a few generations, the darker peppered moths became more common than the lighter ones. In this way, the species adapted to a change in its environment (the air pollution). Now that air pollution has been reduced in England, light-colored peppered moths are becoming more common.

ADAPTATION can make unrelated animals look more alike. The faces of kangaroos and deer, for example, look quite similar because these animals occupy the same niche (although on different continents). They both have long faces with lots of teeth for grinding up the woody vegetation they eat.

LOOK UP: Camouflage, Ecology, Evolution

Air

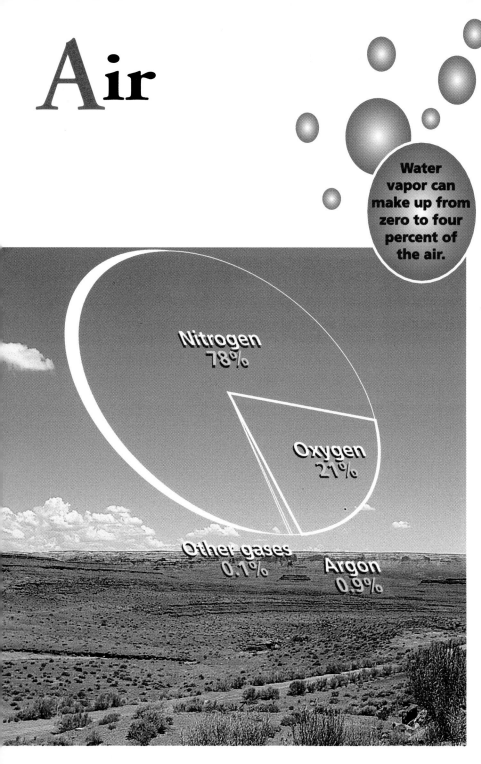

Nitrogen 78%

Oxygen 21%

Other gases 0.1%

Argon 0.9%

Water vapor can make up from zero to four percent of the air.

At sea level, the weight of the air pressing down on Elmo is about one thousand pounds.

AIR IS THE MIXTURE OF GASES THAT MAKE UP THE ATMOSPHERE.

AIR COMPLETELY surrounds the earth. Unpolluted air is invisible and has no smell. But you can feel it when the wind blows, and you can watch it make bubbles when you blow through a straw into a glass of water.

Sometimes air is dry. At other times—just before a storm, for example—air carries lots of water vapor.

CONTENTS

About three-quarters of air is the gas nitrogen. The next most common gas is oxygen, which makes up about one-fifth of the air. A gas called argon is the third most common element, but there is much less of it than of nitrogen and oxygen.

Carbon dioxide makes up just three-ten-thousandths of the air. Other gases in the air include small amounts of krypton, neon, xenon, helium, hydrogen, sulfur dioxide, and carbon monoxide.

Some of these gases are the result of pollution. Breathing carbon monoxide, which comes from car exhaust, can kill humans. Sulfur dioxide, which is produced by burning coal, causes acid rain.

Because drag works against objects moving at high speeds, automobile makers test new car designs in wind tunnels. Inside wind tunnels, air blows over models of cars to show wind drag. Wind tunnels help engineers design cars that are less affected by drag.

Moving air turns the blades of windmills.

The normal air pressure at sea level is 14.7 pounds per square inch. The farther up a person or an object moves into the atmosphere, the less the air pressure. For instance, the air pressure on a mountaintop is only half that at sea level.

AIR PRESSURE
Air itself is light, but the atmosphere is hundreds of miles thick and therefore heavy. The force with which the atmosphere pushes down on a place is called its air pressure.

DRAG
The molecules of a gas are much more spread out than those of a solid. Because of this, objects move easily through air. However, air molecules do drag against objects moving through them.

The larger the object, the greater the drag. Parachutes work because the air beneath the parachute resists the skydiver's fall.

OXYGEN CYCLE
Animals, including humans, need to breathe air in order to stay alive. Their bodies exchange oxygen for carbon dioxide, which their cells give off as waste.

During photosynthesis, plants take in carbon dioxide from the air and use it to make food. They give off oxygen as a waste—oxygen that animals can use.

Barometers measure air pressure. The simplest barometers are glass tubes placed upside down in mercury. When air pressure increases, the air pushes down harder on the mercury and forces some into the tube. This makes the mercury rise inside the tube. When the air pressure drops, mercury flows back out of the tube.

Amphibians

Frogs lay jelly-covered eggs called spawn that float in the water.

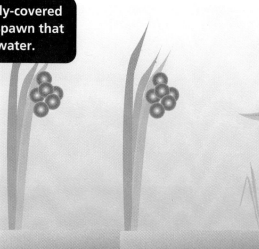

AMPHIBIANS ARE ANIMALS THAT LIVE BOTH IN WATER AND ON LAND.

AMPHIBIANS HATCH FROM eggs laid in water or in other moist places. Adult frogs usually breathe air through lungs and have moist skin.

Because amphibians are cold-blooded animals, the temperature of their bodies changes with their surroundings. They are also vertebrates, which means that they have a backbone.

EVOLUTION

Amphibians were the first vertebrates to leave the sea and spend some time on land. They took this important evolutionary step about 370 million years ago. Biologists believe that amphibians, which evolved from fish, adapted to life on land because food was easy to find there. On land there were also fewer predators to attack them.

MOIST SKIN

Amphibians do not have hair, feathers, or scales. Instead, their skin is naked and smooth. They live in or near the water because they need to keep their skin moist at all times.

Amphibians drink a little, but they take in most of their water through their skin. To help them keep their bodies moist, amphibians cover themselves with a slimy substance called mucus.

TYPES

Scientists divide amphibians into three groups. One includes frogs and toads. Another includes newts and salamanders. The third is made up of wormlike creatures called caecilians, which live in tropical climates.

Frogs have compact tailless bodies and powerful hind legs that allow them to jump great distances. Toads look like frogs, but their skin is drier and rougher because they spend more time out of the water. Toads also have shorter legs. They move by walking, while frogs usually hop.

Newts and salamanders have longer bodies and shorter legs than frogs and toads. They also have tails. Most newts have smooth, slimy skin like that of frogs. Most salamanders have drier, rougher skin like that of toads.

The pouch of skin under a male FROG's mouth is called its vocal sac. When the vocal sac is filled with air, it makes the frog's croaking louder. Male frogs croak during breeding to attract their mates. Each species of frog has its own mating call.

> When tadpoles are about six weeks old, they begin to grow hind legs.

> Newly hatched tadpoles live like fish. They breathe through gills and eat algae. They use long tails to help them swim.

> By the time tadpoles are a few weeks old, their front legs have appeared and their tails have begun to shrink. Sometime during the next month, lungs will replace their gills and they will make the move onto land.

◀▽▲▽◣◢▲▽▲◁▽◁

METAMORPHOSIS

The life cycle of the amphibian re-creates its prehistoric move from water to land. When it comes time to breed, however, most adult amphibians return to the water, where they lay their eggs, called spawn.

The spawn hatch in the water, where the newborn amphibians spend their first few months of life. While they are living in the water, young amphibians go through a metamorphosis. During this process, the newborns change shape and develop the legs and lungs that will allow them to live as adults on land.

Frogs, for example, begin their lives as fishlike tadpoles. The tadpoles slowly lose their tails and grow legs as they develop into adult frogs.

NEWT • In cold weather, warm-blooded animals such as mammals must eat frequently to stay warm. Energy from the food replaces energy used up by their bodies. Cold-blooded amphibians, however, do not have to eat frequently, even in chilly water. They remain comfortable and conserve energy as their body temperature drops.

CAECILIANS, which live both on land and in the water, lay eggs that hatch into tadpoles.

LOOK UP: Adaptation, Biology, Evolution, Life Cycles

Animals

ANIMALS ARE LIVING THINGS THAT EAT FOOD. THEY CAN ALSO MOVE ABOUT DURING AT LEAST ONE STAGE OF THEIR LIVES.

PLANTS MAKE THEIR OWN food, but animals depend on other living things for the food they eat. Animals that eat plants are called herbivores. Those that eat other animals are called carnivores. Those that eat both plants and animals are called omnivores.

DIVERSITY

Scientists have recorded more than 1.5 million different species of animals, but no one knows exactly how many there are. New ones are being discovered all the time, so it is hard for scientists to keep an accurate count.

Animal species are generally grouped into one of two categories: vertebrates or invertebrates. Vertebrates have a backbone. They include fish, birds, amphibians, reptiles, and mammals. Invertebrates do not have a backbone. They include insects, worms, clams, and crabs.

The noisiest land animal is the HOWLER MONKEY. The screams of the howler monkey can be heard up to three miles away.

The longest-living animal is the GIANT TORTOISE. Some giant tortoises have lived nearly two hundred years.

The tallest land animal is the GIRAFFE. It can grow as tall as eighteen feet. Giraffes use their long necks to feed on the leaves of tall trees.

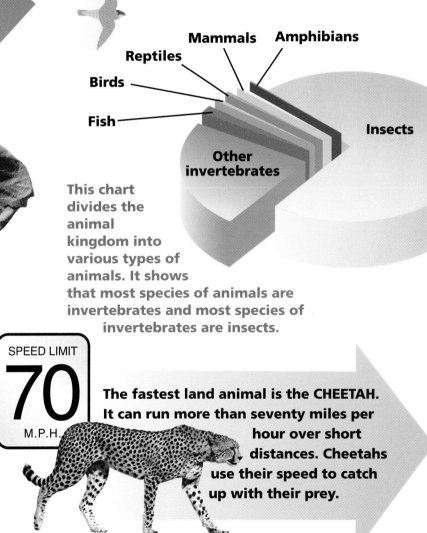

The fastest animal is the SPINETAIL SWIFT. Flying level, it can reach speeds of up to 105 miles per hour. When diving, however, the peregrine falcon can reach a speed of 224 miles per hour.

The largest animal is the BLUE WHALE. It grows more than one hundred feet long and weighs more than one hundred tons.

Mammals **Amphibians**

Reptiles

Birds

Fish

Insects

Other invertebrates

This chart divides the animal kingdom into various types of animals. It shows that most species of animals are invertebrates and most species of invertebrates are insects.

The largest land animal is the AFRICAN ELEPHANT. Male African elephants grow nearly twelve feet tall and weigh up to seven tons.

SPEED LIMIT
70
M.P.H.

The fastest land animal is the CHEETAH. It can run more than seventy miles per hour over short distances. Cheetahs use their speed to catch up with their prey.

LOOK UP: Adaptation, Biology

Astronomy

Many objects in the universe send out radio waves, which can be collected on Earth using a radio telescope. The world's largest radio telescope is located in ARECIBO, PUERTO RICO. Its giant dish collects radio waves just as an optical telescope collects light. Computers translate these waves into pictures.

ASTRONOMY IS THE STUDY OF OBJECTS IN THE UNIVERSE BEYOND EARTH.

ANCIENT ASTRONOMY

Astronomy is the oldest science. From earliest times, people have watched the sky and kept records of what they saw. Early astronomers used the regular movement of stars and planets to make calendars, steer ships at night, and even predict eclipses.

One of the most important early astronomers was Ptolemy, who lived in the Egyptian city of Alexandria during the second century. Ptolemy believed incorrectly that Earth was the center of

Ptolemy

the universe. In 1514, a Polish priest named Nicolaus Copernicus correctly concluded that Earth actually revolved around the Sun.

GALILEO

Another great advance in astronomy came in 1608, when Dutch eyeglass maker Hans Lippershey invented the telescope. Hearing of Lippershey's invention, Italian astronomer Galileo Galilei built his own telescope.

Galileo was able to produce a magnification of about thirty-two times. This means that objects appeared thirty-two times larger in Galileo's telescope than they did to the unaided eye.

Using his telescope, Galileo was able to find in the night sky objects that no

One problem faced by astronomers on Earth is the planet's atmosphere. Observatories are usually built on top of mountains, where there is less atmosphere between the telescope and space. But even on clear nights, the air can still blur the view of these telescopes. The HUBBLE SPACE TELESCOPE orbits in space above the atmosphere. It can see galaxies whose light is too faint to reach Earth's surface.

human being had seen before. Galileo's discoveries included the existence of craters on the Moon, sunspots, and four moons orbiting the planet Jupiter.

MODERN ASTRONOMY

Today, the most advanced modern telescopes include the Arecibo radio telescope, which detects radio waves, and the Hubble Space Telescope.

Astronomers also use space probes to learn more about our solar system. Beginning in 1962, the National Aeronautics and Space Administration (NASA) sent Mariner probes to Venus, Mars, and Mercury.

In 1977, NASA sent two Voyager probes to explore

the giant planets Jupiter, Saturn, Uranus, and Neptune. As the Voyager probes flew by these planets, they sent back radio signals that computers translated into pictures.

DISTANCE

Distances in space are so huge that they have to be measured in extremely large units. One common measure is the astronomical unit (AU), which is equal to ninety-three million miles, or the

average distance between Earth and the Sun.

Another measure is the light year, which is the distance a ray of light travels in one year. Because light travels at 186,000 miles per second, one light year is nearly six trillion miles long.

In numeral form, that would be 6,000,000,000,000 miles.

The star closest to Earth, not including the Sun, is Proxima Centauri, which is 4.3 light years away. The light we see today from that star left Proxima Centauri more than four years ago.

Imagine that you had a telescope powerful enough to see what was happening on Proxima Centauri. Through that imaginary telescope you would see events that happened more than four years ago. In a way, you would be looking backward in time.

Although most space probes use solar power, the VOYAGER probes were nuclear powered because NASA planned to send them to planets where the sunlight was very weak. When VOYAGER 2 flew by Neptune, for example, it was already 2.8 billion miles from the Sun.

LOOK UP: Atmosphere, Energy, Radio, Solar System, Space Flight, Stars, Universe

Atmosphere

Above the mesosphere is the **THERMOSPHERE**, where there is almost no air. In the highest portion of the thermosphere, called the **EXOSPHERE**, some gas molecules escape into space.

The **MESOSPHERE** extends from the top of the stratosphere to fifty miles above the earth. When meteors enter the atmosphere, most burn up in the mesosphere, but some fall to the ground.

The **STRATOSPHERE** extends from the top of the troposphere to thirty miles above the earth. It includes the ozone layer, which is about fifteen miles high. Planes sometimes climb into the lower stratosphere to avoid rough weather in the troposphere.

The **TROPOSPHERE** is the layer of the atmosphere closest to the earth in which most of the world's weather occurs. Depending on weather conditions, the top of the troposphere can be four to eleven miles high.

THE ATMOSPHERE IS THE LAYER OF AIR AROUND THE EARTH. THE EARTH'S GRAVITY HOLDS IT IN PLACE.

THE ATMOSPHERE absorbs the heat of the sun's rays and warms the earth like a blanket. It also absorbs many of the sun's dangerous rays. The part of the atmosphere that blocks out harmful ultraviolet radiation is called the ozone layer.

The atmosphere contains a mixture of gases that we call air. It also contains water and tiny dust particles. Other planets have atmospheres, but these atmospheres contain different mixtures of gases.

THICKNESS

The earth's atmosphere extends more than four hundred miles above its surface. However, compared to the size of the earth, the atmosphere is not very thick. If the earth were an orange, the atmosphere would be its peel.

There is no definite edge to the atmosphere. Instead, the air gets thinner and thinner until the atmosphere disappears into space.

BLUE SKY

During the day, we see blue sky instead of stars because of sunlight. When sunlight passes through the atmosphere, it bounces off air molecules and scatters. Because blue light scatters more than the light of other colors, the sky appears blue.

22 **LOOK UP:** *Air, Gravity, Light and Color, Ozone Layer, Wind*

Atoms and Molecules

Protons and neutrons are much bigger and heavier than electrons. They make up almost all of an atom's mass.

ATOMS ARE THE SMALLEST PIECES OF AN ELEMENT. IF AN ATOM IS BROKEN DOWN, IT IS NO LONGER THAT ELEMENT.

ATOMS ARE VERY TINY. This sheet of paper, for example, is millions of atoms thick.

SUBATOMIC PARTICLES

Atoms are made up of even-smaller parts called protons, neutrons, and electrons. Protons and neutrons form the center, or nucleus, of an atom.

Most of the atom is empty space. Electrons move very rapidly through the space around the nucleus.

MOLECULES

Atoms often join together to form molecules. A molecule may be made up of just two atoms or millions of them.

The number and kinds of atoms in a molecule depend on the substance. For example, a water molecule is made up of three atoms: two atoms of hydrogen and one

atom of oxygen. A molecule of table sugar, however, is made up of forty-five atoms: twelve atoms of carbon, twenty-two atoms of hydrogen, and eleven atoms of oxygen.

Electrons move at nearly the speed of light.

Atoms are mostly empty space, but their electrons move so fast that the atoms seem solid.

LOOK UP: Chemistry, Density, Electricity, Matter, Radioactivity

Backyard

BACKYARD ECOSYSTEMS ARE DOMINATED BY THE PEOPLE WHO LIVE THERE.

◄▶▲▼◄▲▼▲▶◄▼

BACKYARD ECOSYSTEMS are the places in which humans have the most contact with wild animals. They are created when suburbs expand into wild habitats.

The ways in which humans change these habitats benefit some species while harming others. The ones that can adapt to life among humans have an advantage over those that cannot.

◄▶▲▼◄▲▼▲▶◄▼

SUBURBAN EXPANSION

When people move into a wild habitat, they often change important landscape features.

They cut down trees, for example, replacing forests with open lawns. This destroys the habitats of birds and other forest animals, forcing them to find new homes.

Changing existing habitats destroys some niches and creates others. Plants and animals that can adapt, thrive. Others may disappear. Large predators in particular, such as bears and mountain lions, are driven off or killed.

In suburbs across North America, people have killed many of the predators that once killed deer. This has caused the deer to overpopulate and has led to

conflict with humans, who do not want hungry deer raiding their gardens.

◄▶▲▼◄▲▼▲▶◄▼

HABITAT AND FOOD

Human communities provide many places for animals to live. Ledges, storm drains, barns, and chimneys are just a few. Humans also provide an abundance of food, both intentionally and unintentionally. Bird seed in feeders, garden vegetables, flowers, and garbage provide more than enough food for many animals to survive.

1 • BLUE JAY
Blue jays, along with crows and other highly adaptable birds, often prosper in the suburbs at the expense of songbirds.

2 • COTTONTAIL RABBIT The removal of large predators from backyard ecosystems has led to a population explosion among their former prey, particularly cottontail rabbits.

3 • RACCOON
Raccoons are well adapted to backyard life because they will eat almost anything, including food scraps in garbage cans.

4 • HOMEOWNER
Mowing grass and applying insecticides can wipe out insects that many birds depend on for food.

5 • WHITE-TAILED DEER
White-tailed deer like to eat flowers and vegetables. They also carry ticks, whose bites can spread disease.

6 • HOUSE SPARROW
House sparrows build their nests in the eaves of suburban houses.

7 • CAT
Domesticated cats are not native to the suburbs, but they have become one of the top predators in the backyard ecosystem.

LOOK UP: Adaptation, Ecology, Food Chain

Biology

BIOLOGY IS THE STUDY OF LIVING THINGS. IT INCLUDES HOW LIVING THINGS ARE PUT TOGETHER AND HOW THEY BEHAVE.

SOME SCIENTISTS THINK there are more than twenty million different types of plants and animals living on the earth. Biologists have discovered and named about two million species so far. At least three hundred thousand of those species are different types of beetles.

To name living things, biologists use a system called taxonomy. Taxonomic names are written in Latin, which is the language of biology all over the world.

TAXONOMY

Living things are divided into five kingdoms: plants, animals, fungi, protists, and monerans. These last two kingdoms are made up of mainly single-celled microscopic organisms. They include bacteria and some algae. Fungi include mushrooms and molds. They break down dead organic matter into soil.

Within kingdoms, living things are further subdivided into phyla. Phyla are broken down into classes, classes into orders, and orders into families. The divisions within each family include genus and species.

These divisions are part of the taxonomy of every living thing. However, most living things are usually known simply by their genus and species names. For example, biologists call the grizzly bear *Ursus horribilis*, which means "horrible bear" in Latin.

BRANCHES OF BIOLOGY

Within biology, there are many different areas of study. Zoology is the study of animals. Botany is the study of plants. Anatomy is the study of how bodies are put together. Genetics is the study of how traits, such as hair color, are passed on from one generation to the next.

KINGDOM: Animalia

THE ANIMAL KINGDOM has more identified species than any other kingdom.

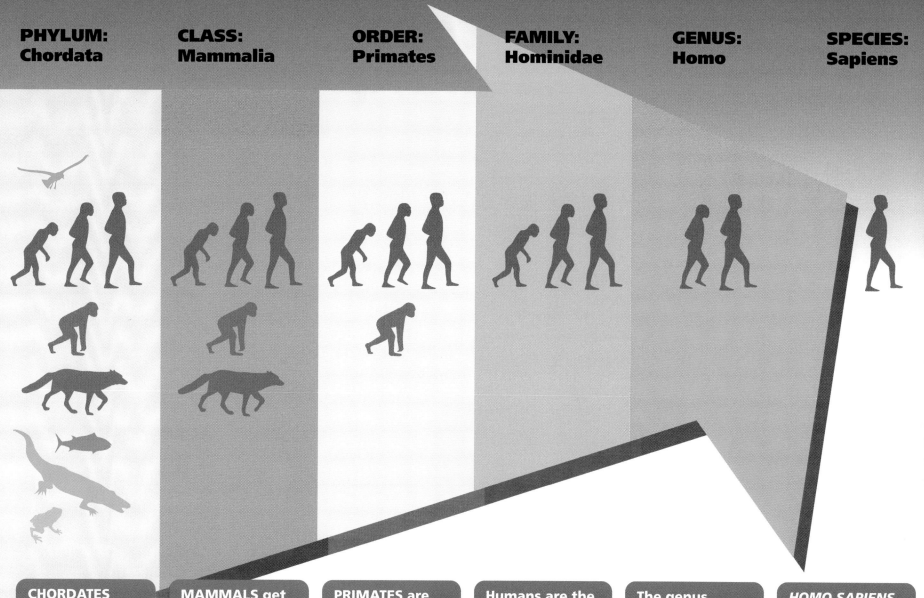

PHYLUM:
Chordata

CLASS:
Mammalia

ORDER:
Primates

FAMILY:
Hominidae

GENUS:
Homo

SPECIES:
Sapiens

CHORDATES are the most advanced animals. They include fish, amphibians, reptiles, birds, and mammals.

MAMMALS get their name from the Latin word for "breast" because female mammals nurse their young with breast milk.

PRIMATES are mammals with large brains and thumbs that allow their hands to grip.

Humans are the only HOMINIDS that still exist today. Others have been identified through the study of fossils.

The genus HOMO includes humans and their recent ancestors, such as *Homo habilis* and *Homo erectus*.

HOMO SAPIENS means "wise man" in Latin.

LOOK UP: Animals, Genetics, Microscopic Life, Plants

Birds

BIRDS ARE THE ONLY ANIMALS WITH FEATHERS. THEY ALSO HAVE WINGS AND BEAKS.

BIRDS LIVE ALMOST everywhere in the world. There are more than nine thousand different species.

Like humans, birds are warm-blooded, which means that their body temperature remains about the same even as the air temperature changes.

Fossils show that birds evolved from early reptiles. Like reptiles, birds are vertebrates, which means that they have a backbone. Also like reptiles, birds lay eggs with a hard shell.

FEATHERS

Feathers are light but strong. In addition to their uses in flight, feathers protect birds from bad weather and help camouflage, or hide, them. A bird's feathers are also called its plumage.

A bird preens itself by using its beak to comb and clean its feathers. Most birds shed their feathers once or twice a year before growing new ones.

Male PEACOCKS use their colorful feathers to attract female peacocks during mating season.

HUMMINGBIRDS have long, pointed beaks that help them suck the nectar from inside flowers. They get their name from the rapid beating of their wings, which makes a humming sound.

BEAKS

While other animals use their jaws and teeth to eat, birds use their beaks. Different birds have different types of beaks depending on the food they eat.

Ducks eat tiny water plants, so they have long beaks for taking in and straining pond water. Eagles have sharp, hooked beaks that help them tear the flesh off the small animals they eat. Robins have pointed beaks, which are useful for picking worms out of the soil. Birds also use their beaks to carry things and to build nests.

MATING

Most birds mate during the spring. Some male birds use their songs to attract females. The males of other species use brightly colored plumage. Some male birds have showy feathers only during mating season. The puffin likewise sheds its brightly colored beak after it mates.

Some birds change mates every season. Others, such as the swan, mate for life.

The first living thing known to have feathers was the ARCHAEOPTERYX, which lived 150 million years ago. Fossilized remains show that it also had claws and a bony tail. These features have led scientists to conclude that its ancestors were reptiles.

There are many different types of feathers. Each type has its own purpose. Wing and tail feathers used in flight are long and strong. The body feathers closest to a bird's skin, called down, are smaller and softer. They keep the bird warm and dry.

EGGS AND NESTS

Birds' nests vary in shape, size, and construction. Woodland birds, for example, build cup-shaped nests. They collect the materials they need one piece at a time.

Dried grass and leaves form the basic shape of the nest, feathers and animal fur keep it warm and dry, lichen helps hide the nest from other animals, and cobwebs hold it all together.

Eggs also come in many different shapes and sizes, as well as colors. Some birds lay just one egg, while others lay many. Birds sit on their eggs to keep them warm until they hatch.

SPEED LIMIT
40
M.P.H.

All birds have wings, but not all birds fly. The OSTRICH, which is the largest bird, cannot fly. However, it can run as fast as forty miles per hour.

Elmo can run about six miles per hour.

Brain

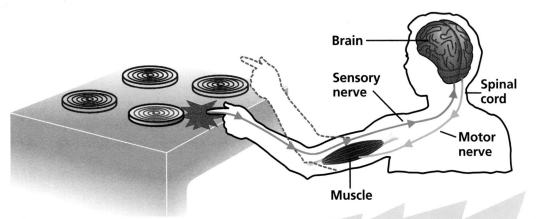

Brain

Sensory nerve

Spinal cord

Motor nerve

Muscle

THE BRAIN IS THE ORGAN THAT CONTROLS ALL OF YOUR BODY'S FUNCTIONS. IT IS PART OF YOUR NERVOUS SYSTEM.

THE HUMAN BRAIN weighs about three pounds and feels like gelatin. Because it is fragile, it needs the hard bones of the skull to protect it.

INVOLUNTARY ACTIONS

The brain controls most important body functions automatically. Actions that you do not have to think about are called involuntary.

For example, to breathe, you do not think about breathing. It just happens.

VOLUNTARY ACTIONS

Other actions, such as brushing your teeth, require that you think about them. These are called voluntary actions.

Your nervous system controls both voluntary and involuntary actions. It receives signals from all parts of your body. Then it sends back more signals telling your muscles whether to expand or contract.

NEURONS

Messages to and from your brain travel back and

REFLEXES are automatic responses that protect your body. If you touch a hot stove, for example, your hand pulls away even before you think about it. When you touch the stove, a sensory neuron in your hand feels the heat and reports it to your spinal cord. Your spinal cord then sends a message back along a motor neuron to one of your muscles. This return message tells the muscle to contract quickly, pulling your hand away. A second later, your brain senses the pain.

forth along a network of nerve cells, or neurons. The brain itself is made up of billions of neurons.

Neurons run from your brain down the center of your back along your spinal cord. From the spinal cord, they branch out all over your body.

Cerebrum

DIFFERENT PARTS OF THE BRAIN control different body functions. The brain stem controls vital body functions, including breathing and heart rate. The cerebellum handles muscle coordination and balance. The cerebrum, the largest and most complicated part of your brain, controls voluntary movement. It also takes care of thinking, learning, and making decisions.

Cerebellum

Brain stem

Camouflage

CAMOUFLAGE IS COLORING AND PATTERNING THAT MAKES A PLANT OR AN ANIMAL BLEND INTO ITS SURROUNDINGS.

Some animals make use of a combination of camouflage techniques. LEOPARDS have spots that match the dotted shade of the forests in which they live. They also lie flat against tree branches when they do not wish to be seen.

PREDATORS USE camouflage to hunt. Prey use camouflage to hide from predators.

BACKGROUND MATCHING

Animal species have developed different forms of camouflage to help conceal them from predators. When an animal's skin color closely matches its surroundings, this is called background matching. Animals that camouflage themselves in this way are often mistaken for objects such as rocks, leaves, and twigs.

Amphibians use background matching to help them avoid predators such as snakes and birds. Dark-green frog skin matches the color of pond water, while the muddy brown skin of toads blends well with the colors of dry leaves and earth.

Some predators, such as polar bears, also use background matching to conceal themselves. Because polar bears' white fur matches the color of snow, seals often do not see them coming until they are close enough to attack.

CONFUSING PATTERNS

Unusual skin patterns, such as stripes and spots, are another type of camouflage. These patterns are called disruptive coloration because they confuse the predator or prey.

Tiger stripes are an example of disruptive coloration. Tigers hunt in fields of long grass. When seen against this background, the tiger's stripes help break up its outline. The swaying grass also hides the tiger's movements.

CHAMELEONS can change color at will, usually in less than two minutes. Besides changing color to hide themselves from predators, chameleons do so when threatening rivals and attracting mates.

Chemistry

The most common elements in Elmo's body are carbon, hydrogen, and oxygen.

CHEMISTRY IS THE STUDY OF THE ELEMENTS AND THE COMPOUNDS THEY MAKE.

The earliest chemists were known as alchemists. Their main goal was to find a way to turn lead into gold. Although alchemists were not scientists in the modern sense, they did develop many of modern chemistry's most basic techniques.

ELEMENTS ARE PURE substances. Therefore, the atoms of a single element are all of one type. For instance, pure oxygen contains only oxygen atoms.

ELEMENTS

The ancient Greek philosopher Aristotle taught that there were four elements: earth, air, fire, and water. He thought these four elements combined in different ways to form all other substances.

Chemists today know that ninety-two elements are found in nature. At least seventeen more have been made by scientists.

CHEMICAL SYMBOLS

Elements are often represented by symbols of one or two letters. For instance, F is the symbol for fluorine and Fe stands for iron. (The letters *Fe* come from *ferrum*, the Latin name for iron.)

Chemists use symbols as shorthand in formulas and equations that show chemical reactions. NaCl is the formula for sodium chloride, or salt. It stands for a compound with one sodium (Na) atom and one chlorine (Cl) atom.

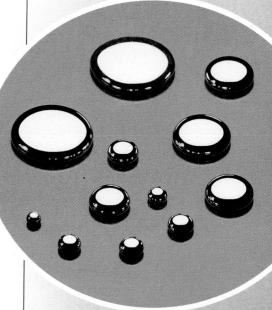

GOLD is one of the few elements found in nature in a pure state. This gold nugget is from Victoria, Australia.

COMPOUNDS

Very few elements exist in nature in a pure state, although there are some exceptions, such as gold and silver. Instead, elements usually occur in compounds. Compounds are two or more elements that have joined together.

Water is a compound made of the gases hydrogen and oxygen. One molecule of water is made of two hydrogen atoms joined to a single oxygen atom (symbol H_2O). A molecule of the compound carbon dioxide (CO_2) contains a single carbon atom bonded to two oxygen atoms.

MIXTURES

A mixture is made of substances that can be separated easily. For example, salt water is a mixture of salt and water.

You can separate the salt from the water by boiling the salt water until the water evaporates. Water, a compound, is much harder to separate into oxygen and hydrogen.

CHEMICAL REACTIONS

Chemical reactions change substances into new ones. For instance, bakers use chemical reactions to turn raw dough into bread. Other chemical reactions inside your body turn that bread into nutrients your cells can use.

MERCURY, which is used in thermometers, and bromine are the only two elements that occur as liquids at room temperature.

Climate

CLIMATE DESCRIBES THE TYPICAL WEATHER OF A REGION.

WEATHER CHANGES FROM one day to the next. It can rain today, be hot tomorrow, and be cool the next day.

Climate is the sum of a region's weather over an entire year. It describes whether a region is generally rainy or dry, warm or cool, sunny or cloudy. Climates sometimes change, too, but much more slowly than weather.

The Sahara desert in Africa has a hot, dry climate. Southern Florida has a hot, humid climate. The Pacific Northwest has a cool, rainy climate.

FACTORS

The factors that scientists use to describe a region's climate include its height above sea level, seasonal temperatures, and average annual rainfall.

Another factor in climate is a region's distance from the EQUATOR. Climates near the equator are warmer than those closer to the earth's poles.

A region's height above sea level, or elevation, is important because air gets cooler as its elevation increases. For this reason, there is always snow on Mount Kenya—even though this extinct African volcano lies near the equator, where the temperature at sea level is always warm.

OCEAN CLIMATE

The ocean has a moderating effect on climate. Areas near the ocean usually have cooler summers and milder winters than areas inland. This is because water warms and cools more slowly than land.

TROPICAL FOREST CLIMATE: The weather in the tropics is extremely hot and usually rainy all year. It changes very little from winter to summer.

TEMPERATE CLIMATE: The world's temperate zones have warm summers, cool winters, and moderate rainfall all year.

COOL FOREST CLIMATE: This climate exists only in the Northern Hemisphere, where pines and other conifers grow. Cool forest climates have short cool summers and long cold winters.

DESERT CLIMATE: Because deserts get very little rain and have few clouds, days there are very hot and nights are very cold. Without clouds in the sky, there is nothing to block out the sun during the day or hold the sun's warmth at night once the ground cools.

POLAR CLIMATE: Polar regions, which are covered with ice and snow, are cold all year.

Clouds

CLOUDS FORM WHEN WATER VAPOR CONDENSES IN THE ATMOSPHERE.

WATER VAPOR IS A GAS. Air nearly always has some water vapor in it.

When the air temperature goes down, some of that water vapor condenses, or turns into a liquid. At first, it forms very small droplets. Clouds are collections of these water droplets in the air.

WEATHER

Clouds affect the weather. In very moist clouds, water droplets combine and get larger. When they finally become too heavy, they fall to the ground as rain or snow.

Clouds also affect the air temperature. During the day, cloud cover can cool the air by blocking out the rays of the sun. During the night, it can act as an insulator, trapping the heat of the earth.

TYPES

Different shapes of clouds form at different altitudes, or heights above the earth. There are three main types:

cirrus, cumulus, and stratus. Other clouds are combinations or variations of these three types.

Clouds sometimes form very low in the atmosphere when warm, humid air comes into contact with cold ground. These conditions produce fog, mist, dew, and sometimes frost.

CIRRUS clouds are thin and wispy. They contain frozen water droplets because they form at high altitudes where the air is cold. They indicate rain is coming.

CUMULUS clouds have flat bottoms and puffy tops. They often form on warm summer days in the middle of the troposphere, the atmosphere layer where weather occurs.

STRATUS clouds form closest to the ground. They can build up in layers or group together in sheets that cover hundreds of square miles.

Dry winds

Moist winds

Rain forest

Clouds often form on the ocean side of mountains near the coast. The height of the mountains forces moist air into higher, cooler altitudes. As the water vapor in the air cools, it condenses. On the far side of the mountains, as the air descends, it warms again and the sky clears.

LOOK UP: Air, Atmosphere, Matter, Rain and Snow, Weather

Coal

COAL IS A COMMONLY USED FUEL MADE FROM FOSSILIZED PLANT REMAINS.

UNTIL ELECTRICITY became widespread during the twentieth century, people used coal to heat their homes and cook their food. Today, some power plants still burn coal to power generators that make electricity.

Coal and oil are called fossil fuels because they are made of the remains of living things. Fossil fuels are called nonrenewable resources because, unlike solar energy, there is a limited supply of them. Once they are used up, they are gone forever.

FORMATION

The coal people use today began to form about 345 million years ago. At that time, great swampy forests filled with trees and huge ferns covered much of the land.

When these trees and ferns died, they fell into the swamps. As the wood and the leaves decayed, they formed a material called peat.

Over millions of years, layers of sediment and rock built up over the peat. Under the weight of tons of rock and water, the peat was eventually compressed into coal.

TYPES

Soft bituminous coal was formed close to the surface.

During the Carboniferous period, SWAMPY FORESTS captured the sun's energy in plants that died and were buried beneath the earth's surface. These dead plants eventually formed coal.

Harder anthracite coal was formed deeper underground.

Anthracite coal is more difficult to mine than bituminous coal. However, it burns much more cleanly. Burning bituminous coal releases into the air many pollutants, some of which cause acid rain.

MINERS dig coal from the earth. Because anthracite coal is so far underground, miners dig vertical shafts several thousand feet deep to reach it.

LOOK UP: Energy, Fossils, Geology, Oil, Pollution, Rocks

Comets and Meteors

COMETS AND METEORS ARE CLUMPS OF MATTER THAT WERE LEFT OVER WHEN OUR SOLAR SYSTEM FORMED.

COMETS

Comets are lumps of ice, rock, and dust that orbit the Sun. Many remain at the distant edge of our solar system. But some comets have orbits that take them quite close to the Sun.

As a comet approaches the Sun, the ice on its surface turns to water and boils away. Gas and dust are released, forming the comet's tail.

Comets are often just a few miles across, but their gas tails can extend for many millions of miles. When all its ice boils away, a comet "dies" and becomes just another orbiting lump of rock.

METEORS

Meteors are bits of rock that cross Earth's path. When they burn up in the atmosphere, people call them "shooting stars." When Earth passes through a cloud of meteors, the spectacular result is called a meteor shower.

Some meteors are too large to burn up completely. Part of them burns away in the atmosphere, but enough remains to reach Earth's surface and make a crater. The part of a meteor that reaches Earth's surface is called a meteorite.

The BARRINGER METEORITE, which landed in Arizona twenty-five thousand years ago, made a crater nearly one mile across. Unlike craters on the Moon, most of those on Earth have weathered away.

LOOK UP: Astronomy, Atmosphere. Moon, Solar System

Computers

Most **PERSONAL COMPUTER** systems have a keyboard and a mouse for inputting data, a disk drive where data is stored, a monitor for displaying the information, and a printer. All these devices are part of the system's hardware.

COMPUTERS ARE VERY POWERFUL ELECTRONIC CALCULATING MACHINES.

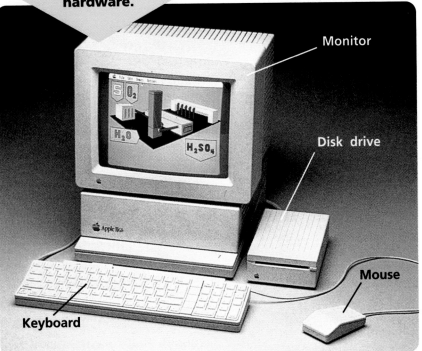

Monitor

Disk drive

Mouse

Keyboard

Apple IIgs

COMPUTERS CARRY OUT many complicated tasks by reducing them to mathematical calculations.

BINARY CODE

Computers work with electrical signals. They can tell whether electrical current is flowing (the "on" state) or not (the "off" state).

Computers use binary numbers to represent these two states. The only digits in binary numbers are 0 and 1. The digit 0 represents the "off" state; the digit 1 represents the "on" state.

Working with rapidly changing combinations of these two digits, computers

Most computers contain several **CIRCUIT BOARDS.**

can represent numbers, letters, and even pictures in binary code. The capital letter C, for example, is written as 01000011 in eight-digit binary code. The number 9 is written as 00001001.

BITS AND BYTES

In the language of computer science, each binary digit is called a bit. An eight-digit binary number is called a byte.

Computer files are usually measured in kilobytes. Each kilobyte is equal to 1,024 bytes.

Early electronic computers used vacuum tubes, which took up a lot of space. The first electronic digital computer, called ENIAC, covered fifteen hundred square feet and weighed thirty tons.

SOFTWARE programs are used to make books like this one.

HARDWARE
Hardware is the name given to the electronic parts of the computer. The most important part, or "brain," of the computer is the central processing unit (CPU).

The CPU, which is located on a circuit board inside the case of the computer, is a tiny microchip. Printed on this chip are hundreds of thousands of miniaturized circuits that control the operations of the computer.

SOFTWARE
The instructions that tell computers what to do are called programs, or software. They are written by computer programmers and often distributed on floppy disks.

Software tells the hardware what to do. A word-processing program is an example of software. So is a video game. Without software, computer hardware would be useless.

APPLICATIONS
Today many electronic appliances contain small computers inside them. For example, small computers called microprocessors control the timers on microwave ovens and the engines in some cars.

LOOK UP: Electricity, Electronics, Mathematics

Continental Drift

CONTINENTAL DRIFT IS THE GRADUAL MOVEMENT OF THE EARTH'S CONTINENTS TOWARD AND AWAY FROM ONE ANOTHER.

PLATE TECTONICS

Scientists do not believe that the solid surface of the earth is all one piece. Instead, they think the land and the oceans rest on huge masses of rock called tectonic plates. Parts of more than one continent can rest on a single plate.

According to the theory of plate tectonics, the earth's plates are constantly moving. Over hundreds of millions of years, continents that once touched one another have slowly moved thousands of miles apart.

LITHOSPHERE

Tectonic plates reach down beyond the rocky crust of the earth to the upper part of the mantle below. The crust and the upper mantle together form the lithosphere. (The word *lithosphere* comes from the Greek word *lithos*, meaning "stone.")

The lithosphere floats on a layer of the mantle that is soft and fluid because it is made of molten rock. Some scientists believe that as the mantle loses heat, it moves, causing the plates to move, too.

PLATE MARGINS

Because tectonic plates are gigantic, the force created by their movement is nearly unstoppable. When the edges of two plates bump into or slide past one another, enormous amounts of pressure are built up and released.

These edges are called plate margins. The margin of the Pacific plate circles all the way from Mexico to Alaska's Aleutian Islands to southern Japan. Most volcanoes and mountain ranges form along plate margins, and most earthquakes also occur there.

The EARTH'S PLATES move only about one inch per year, so changes happen very slowly over hundreds of millions of years.

PANGAEA • Many scientists believe that, at one time, all the continents formed a huge land mass called Pangaea. Two types of evidence support this theory: First, the edges of the continents (as they are today) appear to fit together. For example, Africa's west coast matches the shape of South America's east coast.
The second type of evidence is the fossil record. Fossils of the 250-million-year-old fern *Glossopteris* have been found in Asia, Australia, South America, Africa, and Antarctica. Because fern spores could not have traveled across the ocean, scientists believe these remains indicate the continents were once joined together.

Pangaea as it might have existed two hundred million years ago.

Estimated positions of the continents fifty million years from now.

VOLCANOES

Sometimes when two plates collide, the rocky crust of one plate is slowly pushed down under the leading edge of the other. This often occurs in deep ocean trenches, where oceanic plates meet continental plates.

Because continental plates are less dense, they usually ride over the leading edges of oceanic plates, forcing the oceanic plates down toward the mantle, where they melt and form magma. This magma often pushes back up to the surface through volcanoes. At the same time, at plate margins in the middle of the ocean, new crust is also being formed. Underwater volcanoes along the plate margins bring magma to the surface, where it cools and forms new ocean floor. As proof of this, scientists have shown that the rock in the middle of the ocean is significantly younger than the rock along the shore.

EARTHQUAKES

Sometimes the friction between two colliding plates prevents one from sliding over the other. The pressure that builds up between these two plates causes earthquakes.

Crust

Upper mantle

Lower mantle

Lithosphere

The sea floor moves like the top of a giant conveyor belt— but very slowly.

LOOK UP: Density, Earth, Earthquakes, Fossils, Mountains, Rocks, Volcanoes

Coral Reef

CORAL REEFS FORM IN WARM, SHALLOW OCEAN WATERS.

◄▷△▽◄◄▷△▽△▷◄▽

CORAL REEFS ARE AMONG the world's most productive ecosystems, rivaled only by tropical rain forests. Nearly all the niches in reef ecosystems are filled by one or another brightly colored, oddly shaped creature. Scientists estimate that coral reefs support as many as one-third of the world's fish species.

◄▷△▽◄◄▷△▽△▷◄▽

FORMATION

Although coral reefs look like rock, parts of them are actually alive. Each piece of coral is really a colony of tiny animals called polyps, which are similar to sea anemones.

Like sea anemones, polyps have soft, fleshy bodies and tentacles, which they use to catch their prey. Coral polyps eat microscopic sea animals called zooplankton. Polyps measure between one-sixteenth and one-quarter of an inch long, which is a little smaller than a pencil eraser.

As each polyp grows, it constructs a cup-shaped limestone shell for itself. These limestone shells make up the framework of the coral reef. As old polyps die, new ones build on their remains, and the reef grows. A healthy reef can grow up to one inch every year.

◄▷△▽◄◄▷△▽△▷◄▽

CONDITIONS

Coral polyps grow in warm saltwater where the average surface temperature is about 75° F. Coral also flourishes in shallow water, where sunlight can easily reach algae living among the polyps. These algae are called zooxanthellae.

The symbiotic relationship between the polyps and the zooxanthellae underlies the reef's ecosystem. The zooxanthellae recycle the polyps' waste and use the carbon dioxide for photosynthesis. Also, after the polyps die, the zooxanthellae cement the polyp shells, building the rocklike mass of the reef.

1 • RED-FOOTED BOOBIES hover over coral reefs before diving to catch prey they have spotted. They mostly eat flying fish, which they can pick out of the air.

2 • The slim bodies of these **SURGEON FISH** enable them to move easily through the maze of coral shapes and hide inside crevices when danger threatens.

3 • CORAL shapes vary according to each species of polyp. Tree corals grow in branches that look like tiny underwater trees, while brain corals grow in rounded, grooved masses.

4 • The prickly **CROWN-OF-THORNS STARFISH** poses the greatest danger to coral reefs because it eats living polyps. A recent explosion in the crown-of-thorns population along Australia's Great Barrier Reef has threatened the survival of the entire reef.

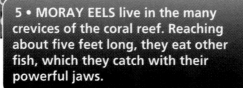

1

6

2

3

5

4

7

5 • MORAY EELS live in the many crevices of the coral reef. Reaching about five feet long, they eat other fish, which they catch with their powerful jaws.

6 • BLACK-TIPPED REEF SHARKS, which can grow up to eight feet long, live along the edges of reefs and feed on the many fish there.

7 • SEA ANEMONES, which are usually just a few inches across, can grow up to three feet wide in the friendly waters of the Great Barrier Reef. Anemones attach themselves to the reef and wait for small fish to pass within striking range of their stinging tentacles.

LOOK UP: Adaptation, Camouflage, Ecology, Food Chain, Microscopic Life, Parasites

Crystals

Crystal molecule

DIAMONDS are crystals of the element carbon.

CRYSTALS ARE SOLIDS WITH REGULAR, FLAT-SIDED SHAPES.

ALMOST EVERY SOLID that occurs in nature is made up of crystals. Crystals of different minerals have different shapes.

Salt looks like rough sand to the unaided eye, but a magnifying glass can show that it is actually made up of small, regular crystals.

Many crystals are transparent. Some, like salt, are small. Others are large enough to be seen very easily.

FORMATION

Some crystals are formed when molten rock cools and hardens. Others are formed when water with minerals dissolved in it evaporates. In both cases, mineral atoms form solids by coming together in regular patterns.

These repeating, regular patterns make crystals both strong and hard. Crystals of the same mineral always follow the same pattern.

A GEODE is a hollow rock inside of which crystals form. This geode contains crystals of the mineral amethyst, which is a type of quartz.

GEMS

Rare and valuable mineral crystals are called gems. Diamonds, rubies, emeralds, and sapphires are all gems. They are often used to make jewelry.

Although scientists can make gems in their laboratories, the ones found in nature are the most valuable. Gems are usually found buried in rocks. They have to be mined before they can be cut, polished, and made into rings or necklaces.

LOOK UP: Atoms and Molecules, Matter, Rocks

Density

DENSITY MEASURES HOW TIGHTLY THE PARTICLES IN A SUBSTANCE ARE PACKED TOGETHER.

THE PARTICLES IN VERY dense substances, such as metal and stone, are very close together. Wood and plastic are much less dense.

FLOTATION

Solid objects float if they are less dense than the liquid around them. For example, surfboards float in water because they are less dense than water. For the same reason, spilled oil floats in the ocean because it is less dense than seawater.

Submarines use this same principle to move up and down in the water. In order to submerge, a sub takes on water, which makes it heavier. This extra weight makes the sub denser than the water around it, so it sinks.

In order to rise, the sub pumps water out, making it lighter. Because the sub is now less dense than the water around it, it rises.

Elements and compounds are usually more dense in their solid states than in their liquid states, but water is an exception. Solid water, or ice, is less dense than liquid water, so ice floats instead of sinking to the ocean bottom.

LOOK UP: Atoms and Molecules, Matter

Desert

DESERTS ARE HABITATS WHERE LITTLE RAIN FALLS AND THE CONDITIONS ARE GENERALLY HARSH.

DESERTS COVER ABOUT one-fifth of the world's land surface. A region is classified as a desert if it receives less than ten inches of rainfall per year.

TEMPERATURE

Most people think of deserts as hot places, but temperatures can vary greatly. Hot deserts can turn quite cold at night because they have no clouds overhead to hold in heat from the day's sunshine.

Other deserts, such as the Antarctic, are cold all the time. The Antarctic qualifies as a desert—the world's largest, in fact—because it receives little rainfall each year.

PLANT ADAPTATION

Desert plants commonly have broad root systems that maximize collection of whatever rainwater does fall. They also have thick, waxy skins and small or no leaves. Both of these traits keep desert plants from losing moisture.

Some desert plants coat their seeds with a chemical that prevents them from sprouting until rains wash the coating away. Before the ground can dry again, these plants mature, flower, and produce their own seeds, passing through an entire life cycle in just two weeks.

ANIMAL ADAPTATION

Desert animal species have also developed ways to conserve water. The kangaroo rat, for example, never sweats. Many desert animals never drink, either. Instead, they get their water from their food.

During the day, most desert animals rest out of the sun, usually in burrows or beneath rocks. Snakes cannot dig burrows them-selves, but they often live in abandoned ones. Sometimes they invade occupied ones, killing and eating their owners.

1 • SAGUARO CACTUS
The spines on this forty-foot-tall saguaro cactus are actually tiny leaves. They protect the saguaro from animals that would otherwise eat its flesh for the water stored there. In these plants, photosynthesis takes place in the green stems.

2 • BARREL CACTUS
Most plants take in carbon dioxide and release oxygen during the day. But the barrel cactus takes in carbon dioxide at night, when the desert is cooler. It stores the carbon dioxide in its cells and uses it for photosynthesis once the sun comes out. This adaptation helps save water.

3 • SCORPION
Scorpions use their tails to inject deadly poison into their prey. This method of hunting uses up much less energy than fighting, which makes it better suited to the desert.

4 • GILA MONSTER
Lizards such as the Gila monster prosper in the desert because their dry, scaly skins resist evaporation. They are cold-blooded, which means they can slow down their bodies' metabolism and save energy.

5 • RATTLESNAKE
Rattlesnakes hunt at night, when desert temperatures are cooler. They use heat-sensitive pits in their faces to locate warm-blooded prey such as the kangaroo rat.

6 • KANGAROO RAT
During the day, kangaroo rats usually stay underground in their burrows. There, the air is moister and up to twenty degrees cooler than the air outside.

7 • CACTUS WREN
Because few, if any, trees grow in the desert, cactus wrens build their nests in the arms of the saguaro cactus. The spines of the saguaro protect the young birds from predators.

LOOK UP: Adaptation, Climate, Ecology, Food Chain, Life Cycles, Plants, Senses

Digestion

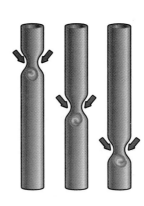

Smooth muscles push food along the alimentary canal. Muscles in the walls of your esophagus, for instance, contract in waves to move food down toward your stomach. These contractions are called PERISTALSIS. They are so strong that you can even swallow food while hanging upside down.

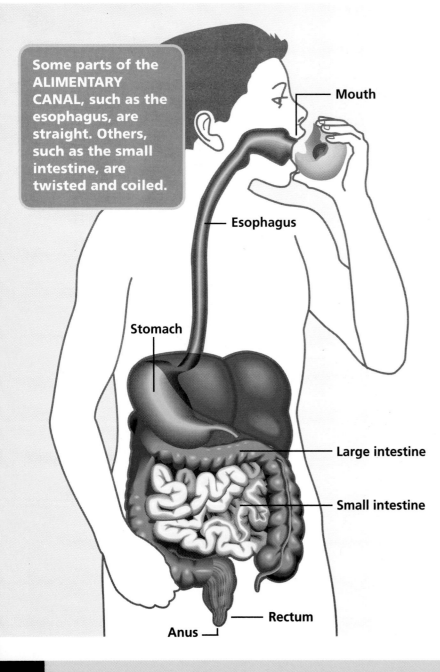

Some parts of the ALIMENTARY CANAL, such as the esophagus, are straight. Others, such as the small intestine, are twisted and coiled.

Mouth

Esophagus

Stomach

Large intestine

Small intestine

Rectum

Anus

DIGESTION IS THE PROCESS BY WHICH HUMANS BREAK DOWN THE FOOD THEY EAT.

DIGESTION BREAKS DOWN your food into pieces small enough to be soaked up by your blood.

ALIMENTARY CANAL

Digestion happens in stages as food travels along a path called the alimentary canal. In adults, the alimentary canal is about twenty-seven feet long.

It can take as long as two days for a meal to pass from one end of your alimentary canal to the other.

MOUTH

The alimentary canal begins in your mouth. As you bite into food, your teeth chop and grind it. Your mouth also mixes your saliva with the food particles.

Your saliva contains digestive juices made up of enzymes. These enzymes break down some of the chemicals in your food as soon as you put it in your mouth. Saliva also makes food slippery so that it can slide down your esophagus more easily.

ESOPHAGUS

The esophagus is the tube that carries food from your

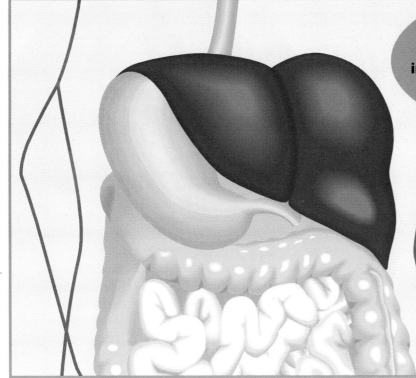

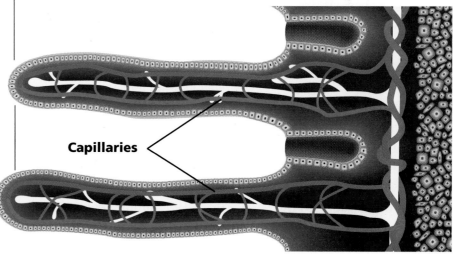

The LIVER is the largest organ inside your body. It makes digestive juices used in the small intestine. It also filters poisons from the bloodstream and breaks down used red blood cells.

long. In the small intestine, food is further broken down into nutrients small enough for your blood to absorb. Your blood then carries these nutrients to the different cells in your body.

Undigested food passes from the small intestine into the large intestine, or colon. There, leftover water soaks back into the bloodstream. The solids that remain pass through your rectum, then out of your body through your anus.

WASTE
However, even after your blood carries away the nutrients, part of the food remains. This is waste that your body cannot use.

VILLI are tiny folds that stick out from the walls of your small intestine. They create a larger area through which nutrients can pass. Nutrients pass through the villi into capillaries, where they are absorbed by the blood.

mouth to your stomach. It is the narrowest part of the alimentary canal.

The stomach is the widest part. It is elastic and can expand when you eat a large meal.

STOMACH
Muscles around your stomach contract and relax. This action churns the food inside, mixing it with even more chemicals.

After half an hour, some of the food moves on to the next

stage of digestion. Other parts stay in your stomach for up to four hours. When the stomach muscles have finally churned and mixed all the food into a paste, it passes through into the small intestine.

SMALL INTESTINE
The small intestine is the longest part of the alimentary canal. In a typical adult, the small intestine is twenty-one feet

Capillaries

LOOK UP: Heart and Blood, Human Body, Muscles, Nutrition, Taste

Dinosaurs

DINOSAURS WERE REPTILES THAT DOMINATED LIFE ON THE EARTH UNTIL THEIR EXTINCTION SIXTY-FIVE MILLION YEARS AGO.

◄▷▲▽▲▷◄▷▲▷◄▽

FOSSIL RECORDS SHOW that dinosaurs first appeared on the earth about 220 million years ago. Other animals lived among them—including fish, amphibians, and even primitive mammals—but dinosaurs were the dominant animals.

◄▷▲▽▲◄▷▲▷◄▽

TYPES

There were hundreds of different species of dinosaurs. Some ate meat and some ate plants. Some walked on two feet and others walked on four.

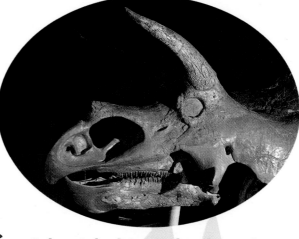

Paleontologists use fossil remains to create drawings of what particular dinosaurs might have looked like. Fossilized skeletons helped create this likeness of a *TRICERATOPS*, but fossils cannot reveal everything. For instance, they cannot tell paleontologists what color a dinosaur's skin may have been or what sounds the animal made.

Not all of these dinosaurs lived at the same time, and not all were the same size. Early dinosaurs, for example, were small. *Coelophysis*, which lived about 210 million years ago, was just six feet tall. It ate small mammals and other reptiles.

Most of the larger dinosaurs lived during the Jurassic period, which lasted from 190 million years ago until the beginning of the Cretaceous period 136 million years ago. *Tyrannosaurus rex* was a large meat-eating dinosaur of the Cretaceous period.

EXTINCTION

Because dinosaur fossils have never been found in rocks less than sixty-five million years old, paleontologists have concluded that dinosaurs became extinct at that time.

Paleontologists think it unusual that all the dinosaurs were wiped out at the same time. Many believe that some extreme change in the earth's climate may have been responsible.

One theory suggests that a large meteorite crashed into the earth at the end of the Cretaceous period, creating a huge cloud of dust that blocked out the sun. Without the sun's heat and light, many plants could not grow and the earth became much colder. Dinosaurs could not have survived under these conditions.

FOSSILS

Although the last dinosaurs died sixty-five million years ago, paleontologists still know a lot about them because of the fossils they left behind. Researchers have found complete fossilized dinosaur skeletons, teeth, eggs, tracks, and even droppings.

When paleontologists study these fossils, they think about what each dinosaur might have looked like and how it might have lived. For example, the shape of a dinosaur's teeth can indicate to a paleontologist what kind of food that animal ate. Sharp, pointed teeth suggest a meat-eater. Dull, rounded teeth probably belonged to a plant-eater.

According to one theory, the EXTINCTION of the dinosaurs was caused by a large meteorite striking the earth.

MODERN RELATIVES

Like modern reptiles, dinosaurs had backbones and scaly skin, and they laid eggs. However, modern reptiles are all cold-blooded, while dinosaurs were probably warm-blooded. Also, some dinosaurs may have traveled in herds, while none of today's reptiles do.

Some paleontologists believe that dinosaurs may also be the ancient relatives of birds. Like dinosaurs, birds lay eggs and travel in groups.

Elmo is about as tall as the knee of the *Apatosaurus.*

Among the giant dinosaurs that lived during the Jurassic period were the sauropods. These plant-eating dinosaurs included the *APATOSAURUS* shown here.

Earth

Earth is the planet on which we live.

USING RADIOACTIVE dating, geologists have calculated that the earth is about 4.6 billion years old.

SHAPE AND SIZE

Although the earth has the general shape of a sphere, it is not completely round. It bulges slightly at the equator and is flattened at the poles.

The diameter of the earth, or the distance through its center, is 7,926 miles at the equator. The earth's circumference, which is the distance around the world at the equator, is 24,901 miles.

LAYERS

The earth is made up of different layers, with lighter material on the outside and heavier matter on the inside. The outermost layer is the atmosphere, which is a layer of air.

The earth's surface layer is called the crust. The thickness of the crust varies from two miles under the ocean to thirty-seven miles under tall mountain ranges. On average, the rock-and-soil crust is about nineteen miles thick.

Beneath the crust is the mantle, and at the center of the earth is the core. Geologists divide the core into two regions: a liquid outer core and a solid inner core, both of which contain iron, nickel, and probably sulfur or silicon.

Atmosphere
400 miles thick

Crust
19 miles thick

Mantle
1,800 miles thick

Outer core
1,300 miles thick

Inner core
1,700 miles across

The mantle and the core are too far down to reach by drilling. Instead, geologists learn about these inner layers by studying how the shock waves produced by earthquakes change as they pass through them.

The axis of the earth tilts about 23.5° in relation to its orbit. This tilt causes the seasons. For half of the year, the Northern Hemisphere leans toward the sun, bringing summer to Europe and the United States and winter to Australia and Brazil. As the earth moves around the sun, however, the tilt brings the Southern Hemisphere closer to the sun, and the seasons are reversed.

LOOK UP: Atmosphere, Continental Drift, Geology, Seasons

Earthquakes

EARTHQUAKES ARE SHOCK WAVES PRODUCED BY SHIFTING TECTONIC PLATES.

CAUSES

The line along which two tectonic plates meet is called a fault. When two plates push against each other, pressure develops along their common fault line.

When too much pressure builds up, the rocks within the plates crack and shift, causing an earthquake. Most earthquakes last less than one minute.

FOCUS

The point at which the shift occurs is the focus of the earthquake. The focus can be near the surface or deep underground. The point on the surface directly above the focus is called the epicenter.

Seismic, or shock, waves created by earthquakes travel out from the focus. These waves are strongest at the epicenter but can be felt all over the world.

In California, the American and Pacific plates slide past each other along the **SAN ANDREAS FAULT.** Scientists estimate that the plates move along the fault at about two and a half inches per year. Most of this movement happens in sudden jumps when the earth shifts quickly.

Fault line

RICHTER SCALE

In 1935, seismologist Charles F. Richter introduced a scale by which earthquakes recorded on a seismograph could be measured and compared.

His Richter scale measures an earthquake's magnitude, or the force that it produces. Each unit on the Richter scale stands for a tenfold increase in magnitude. Therefore, an earthquake measuring 4.7 on the Richter scale is ten times more powerful than one measuring 3.7.

Epicenter

Focus

Seismic waves

Although **EARTHQUAKES** can occur up to 450 miles below the earth's surface, those deeper than 45 miles have little effect on the ground above. The most destructive earthquakes are those with a focus less than six miles deep.

Ecology

ECOLOGY IS THE STUDY OF HOW LIVING THINGS RELATE TO ONE ANOTHER AND TO THEIR ENVIRONMENT.

NO LIVING THING CAN survive on its own. Animals need plants, animals, and other living things for food. Plants need sun, soil, water, and carbon dioxide to grow.

Ecologists try to understand the connections among different living things. They also look at the way living things interact with their environment.

ECOSYSTEMS

Ecologists study ecosystems. An ecosystem is a community made up of living things, such as plants and animals, and the nonliving things that affect them.

Ecologists who study an ecosystem look at how its plants and animals live together. They also observe the soil, the water, the rocks, the geography, and the weather patterns.

Ecosystems can be as small as tidal pools or as large as deserts. Rain forests, coral reefs, and grasslands are all ecosystems. The earth itself can be considered one giant ecosystem.

BALANCE

Ecosystems are healthy when all their parts are in balance. The plants provide food and oxygen for the animals—which, in turn, provide carbon dioxide for the plants. Because all the living things in an ecosystem are interrelated, what happens to one species affects the others.

The balance of an ecosystem can be upset in different ways. Natural

Ecologists study the food chains in an ecosystem to see how the living things link together. They also observe how these living things relate to the climate and landscape.

Red squirrels exhale some of the carbon dioxide that plants use for photosynthesis. They also leave droppings that help fertilize the soil.

Plants, such as this pine tree, are called PRODUCERS because they make their own food.

Red squirrels, which eat the seeds produced by pine trees, are called PRIMARY CONSUMERS because they eat producers directly.

disasters, such as hurricanes and fires, can affect it. But people are the greatest threat to most ecosystems.

HUMAN THREAT

People pollute ecosystems every day with garbage, pesticides, and other poisonous chemical wastes. These may harm only one species at first, but the damage soon reaches others through the food web.

An example of this occurs when rain washes a pesticide off some crops and into a pond, where it kills some small fish. The birds that feed on those fish are left without food, so they either die or, if they can, move away.

Sometimes people damage ecosystems by introducing a new species of plant or animal into the environment.

Australian hunters once imported hares from England. These rabbitlike mammals were supposed to be food for game

RICE PADDY FARMING These are rice farmers in Thailand. Farming is one of the ways in which humans change the ecosystems in which they live.

animals. The hunters thought that making food more available would increase the number of game animals.

Because they had no natural enemies in Australia, the English hares began to

reproduce rapidly. Soon there were so many hares that they ate up nearly all the grass on which the cattle grazed. As a result, the cattle population dropped, leading to a shortage of beef and milk.

Foxes and hawks are called SECONDARY CONSUMERS because they get their energy from eating primary consumers, such as red squirrels. These animals are also called top predators because nothing in the ecosystem eats them.

LOOK UP: Animals, Food Chain, Plants, Pollution

Electricity

Electricity carries messages between your brain and the nerve receptors in your body.

ELECTRICITY THAT YOU USE IN YOUR HOME IS A FORM OF ENERGY. IT IS MADE UP OF ELECTRONS MOVING IN A STREAM.

ELECTRICITY IS THE most practical form of energy because it can be easily changed to other kinds of energy. For example, lamps change electricity into light and electric ovens turn electricity into heat.

CONDUCTORS

Materials through which electricity travels are called conductors. Some materials conduct electricity better than others.

Some metals are very good conductors. That is why most electrical wire is made from copper or aluminum.

INSULATORS

Materials that do not conduct electricity very well are called nonconductors, or insulators. Insulators are used to control electricity and protect people from its charge.

Switches control the flow of electricity through a CIRCUIT by opening and closing the loop.

Plastics make very good insulators. Most power cords are covered with plastic to prevent people who touch them from being shocked.

CIRCUITS

Electricity flows in a loop called a circuit. If the loop is broken, the electricity cannot flow.

Every circuit contains a power source. When the loop is completed, electricity flows from the power source through the circuit. When the power source is a battery, electricity flows from one pole through the circuit and back to the other pole.

CURRENT AND VOLTAGE

Current is the flow of electricity through a circuit. Electrical current is measured in units called amperes.

LIGHTNING is caused by static electricity that builds up within thunder clouds and between the clouds and the ground.

STATIC ELECTRICITY Rubbing two objects together can create static electricity, which is electricity that does not flow. Rubbing a balloon against your sweater can create static electricity that makes the balloon stick to your hand.

When you walk across a rug, static electricity builds up in your body. When you touch a doorknob or someone else, you complete an electrical circuit, current flows, and you feel a small shock.

Electrical force is measured in units called volts. Power lines, for example, have very high voltages. The higher the voltage in a circuit is, the greater its current.

RESISTANCE
Most materials resist the flow of electricity. Material that does not conduct electricity well is said to have high resistance.

In an electrical circuit, resistance is measured in units called ohms.

SUPERCONDUCTORS
There is no such thing as a circuit without any resistance, but scientists are now working on superconductors. These are special materials whose resistance is so low that it cannot be measured.

Many of these superconductors are alloys of metals that are kept at extremely low temperatures.

LOOK UP: Atoms and Molecules, Electronics, Energy, Metals, Rain and Snow

Electronics

The metal tracks printed on the CIRCUIT BOARD connect the different components mounted on the board.

Electronics is the technology that controls electrical currents.

COMPUTERS, calculators, and digital watches are all electronic devices. They produce signals that carry information by controlling the flow of electrons through tiny circuits.

CIRCUIT BOARD

The basic unit of every electronic device is the circuit board. Circuit boards control the flow of electrical current through a machine. By controlling the current very precisely, circuit boards allow electronic machines to perform very complicated tasks.

Circuit boards contain hundreds of components. Each component has its own specific job. In a computer, the most important of these components is the microprocessor, or microchip.

MICROCHIPS can perform as many as one million arithmetic operations per second.

MICROCHIP

The microchip is itself a tiny circuit board. Some microchips are no larger than a ladybug.

A typical microchip contains hundreds of thousands of miniaturized parts. Microchips are usually made from wafer-thin slices of silicon.

LOOK UP: Atoms and Molecules, Energy, Metals, Rain and Snow

Endangered Species

ENDANGERED SPECIES ARE SPECIES OF PLANTS AND ANIMALS CURRENTLY FACING EXTINCTION.

◄▷△▽◄▷△▽▷△▽◄▽

A SPECIES OF PLANT OR animal is considered extinct when it has not been observed in the wild for fifty years. Over the long history of the earth, countless species have become extinct, most notably the dinosaurs. These species usually disappeared as newer species replaced them or because the earth's climate changed.

◄▷△▽◄▷△▽▷△▽◄▽

HUMAN IMPACT

Today, many species are becoming endangered because of human activity. Hunters kill many animals, such as tigers and the great Indian rhinoceros, because

The DODO was a large flightless bird native to the island of Mauritius in the Indian Ocean. Portuguese explorers first sighted a dodo in 1507. By 1681, the dodo was extinct, killed off by European sailors and the dogs and cats they brought with them.

their skins and tusks are valuable. Farmers kill wolves because they think wolves will eat their sheep. When too many animals are killed, their species becomes endangered.

The fact that a species is highly desirable can be the reason it becomes endangered. For example, some people take rare and beautiful plants out of the wild for their own gardens. If they take too many, they can threaten the ability of these species to reproduce.

Most species become endangered when their habitats are threatened. GIANT PANDAS live in the bamboo forests of southwestern China. Recently, these forests have been cleared to make way for rice paddies and villages. As a result, very few pandas remain in the small areas that are left.

◄▷△▽◄▷△▽▷△▽◄▽

CONSERVATION

Biologists conserve endangered animal species in two important ways: First, they preserve and breed specimens in zoos and botanical gardens. Even better, they protect native habitats from overuse by people.

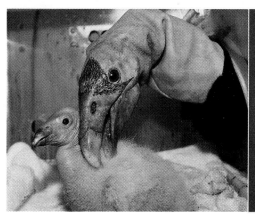

Like many endangered species, the CALIFORNIA CONDOR is difficult to breed in captivity. In the wild, its females lay a single egg just once every two years. In 1983, however, biologists at the San Diego Zoo succeeded in hatching the first California condor chick born in captivity.

Energy

SOLAR ENERGY
The sun is the most important source of energy in the solar system. Most satellites get their power from photoelectric cells that convert sunlight into electricity.

ENERGY CAN CHANGE THE STATE AND POSITION OF MATTER. HEAT, LIGHT, AND SOUND ARE ALL FORMS OF ENERGY.

NUCLEAR ENERGY
The nuclear forces that hold an atom together are amazingly strong. Splitting the atom releases this energy.

FORCE IS PUSH OR PULL. When one object pushes or pulls another, it transfers some of its energy to the other object.

A force that moves matter is doing work. Energy is sometimes defined as the ability to do work.

POTENTIAL

Energy that is stored is called potential energy. For example, jet fuel has a high potential energy. In other words, it has the potential to do a lot of work.

In the tank of an airplane, jet fuel does not perform any work. Burning the fuel, however, causes the plane to move.

KINETIC

The energy of a moving object is called kinetic energy. Burning the jet fuel changes the form of its energy from potential to kinetic.

As more fuel is burned, more potential energy is changed to kinetic energy, and the plane moves faster and faster.

WIND ENERGY • Wind is another source of energy. Before the Industrial Revolution, farmers used windmills to grind their grain and pump water. Today, wind turbines are used to produce electricity.

CONSERVATION

The law of conservation of energy states that energy cannot be created or destroyed. It can only be changed from one form into another.

Energy is constantly changing forms. For instance, when a moving car slows down, its brakes rub against its wheels. The car's kinetic energy changes to heat energy produced by the friction between the brakes and the wheels.

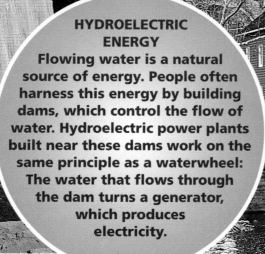

HYDROELECTRIC ENERGY
Flowing water is a natural source of energy. People often harness this energy by building dams, which control the flow of water. Hydroelectric power plants built near these dams work on the same principle as a waterwheel: The water that flows through the dam turns a generator, which produces electricity.

LOOK UP: Atoms and Molecules, Matter, Physics, Sun, Wind

Evolution

EVOLUTION IS THE PROCESS BY WHICH LIVING THINGS CHANGE AND DEVELOP OVER TIME.

RECENT STUDIES HAVE shown that some evolutionary changes, such as a change in the shape of an animal's head, can be seen within a few generations. But the most important evolutionary changes, such as the development of a new species, can take hundreds of millions of years.

EVOLUTIONARY LADDER

For much of its 4.6-billion-year history, the earth was a barren, lifeless place. Among the first living things were single-celled organisms called protists, which began to appear about three billion years ago.

For the next 2.5 billion years, small sea creatures developed. Then 500 million years ago, the first fish appeared. About 370 million years ago, some bony fish grew legs and crawled up onto the land. These were the first amphibians.

The next important group of animals, the reptiles, evolved from the amphibians. Reptiles appeared about 320 million years ago. At first, most reptiles crawled on the ground, but eventually some began to walk on their hind legs. Others developed wings and began to fly.

Australopithecus appeared 4 million years ago.

Homo habilis appeared 2 million years ago.

Homo erectus appeared 1.5 million years ago.

Walking erect was an important evolutionary step for human ancestors.

Mammals appeared about two hundred million years ago when dinosaurs still dominated the earth. The earliest mammals were small furry creatures. From them, time and evolutionary change produced the mammals we know today, including humans.

CHARLES DARWIN

The ancient Greeks were the first people to think about evolution. But British naturalist Charles Darwin developed the first theory of evolution based on scientific observation.

During the 1830s, Darwin sailed to South America, where he visited the

FINCHES on the mainland typically have large, powerful beaks, which they use to crack open hard seed husks. But some of the finches Darwin studied had long, pointed bills, which they used to pick insects out of cracks. Darwin believed that these finches evolved into insect eaters that would not have to compete with seed-eating finches for food.

The similar **BONE STRUCTURES** in a bird's wing, a whale's flipper, and a human arm suggest that all three creatures evolved from a common ancestor.

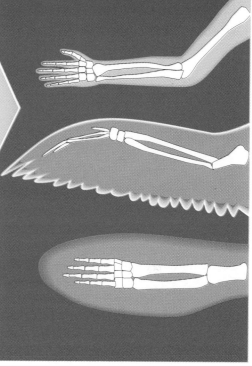

Galápagos Islands and studied the finches there. Because the Galápagos Islands were small and far away from other places, Darwin assumed that the Galápagos finches must have originally flown over from the mainland. This led him to the conclusion that all the different species he found on the islands must have descended from the same ancestors.

◄▼▲▼◄▼►

NATURAL SELECTION

In 1859, Darwin published a book called *On the Origin of Species*, which presented his theory of natural selection. Darwin argued that, over a great deal of time, the original Galápagos finches had changed, or mutated, into different species.

According to Darwin's theory, the most useful changes were passed on to new generations because these birds lived longer and reproduced more often. Meanwhile, harmful mutations were not passed on, because these birds often died before they could reproduce.

Based on his observation of finches, Darwin theorized that all species must evolve in order to meet the demands of a changing environment. According to Darwin's theory, species that were unable to change died out, or became extinct.

Some species, such as the CROCODILE, have evolved little or not at all.

LOOK UP: Adaptation, Geology, Scientific Method

Fish

FISH ARE ANIMALS THAT LIVE UNDERWATER. THEY HAVE GILLS FOR BREATHING, FINS FOR SWIMMING, AND SCALES THAT COVER THEIR SKIN.

◄▷▲▽◄▷▲▽◄▷▲▽

FISH ARE VERTEBRATES, which means they have a backbone. There are over nineteen thousand different species of fish, more than any other group of vertebrates. Fish are cold-blooded, which means their body temperature changes depending on their surroundings.

Most fish live in either freshwater lakes and rivers or saltwater seas. The salmon is one of the few fish that can live in both.

◄▷▲▽◄▷▲▽◄▷▲▽

TYPES

The most common fish have streamlined, bullet-shaped

Some fish, such as the FLOUNDER, have flat bodies. Flounder live on the ocean bottom, where their shape and spotty brown skin allow them to hide in the sand.

bodies and bony skeletons. Others, like sharks, have flexible skeletons made of rubbery tissue called cartilage.

The third group are the jawless fish, which include the lamprey. There are only about seventy species of jawless fish. They look like snakes and feed on other fish.

Fish come in many different sizes. The dwarf pygmy goby is only one-third of an inch long. The whale shark can grow up to fifty feet long.

Very small fish can often escape predators by hiding in the narrow openings between rocks, while very large fish are simply too big for other fish to swallow.

◄▽▲▽◄◄▽▲▽◄▽

GILLS

Fish breathe through their gills. Most fish have four pairs of gills located directly behind their heads. Fish gills are made up of tiny blood vessels.

When fish swim, they swallow water, which is pumped out through their gills. As the water passes through, blood vessels in the gills absorb some of the oxygen that is dissolved in the water.

◄▽▲▽◄◄▽▲▽◄▽

SCALES

Scales are thin, protective plates that cover a fish's skin.

The GREAT WHITE SHARK never stops growing teeth. As its front teeth wear down and fall out, new teeth formed in the back of the jaw move up to take their place.

Many fish travel in groups called SCHOOLS. Schools of fish are often so large that predators have trouble picking out a single fish to attack. Well-coordinated schools of fish can sometimes be mistaken for a single, much larger fish.

They generally overlap like the shingles on a roof. Scales also have an oily coating that helps fish swim by reducing the friction between the scales and the water.

Bony fish have smooth circular scales. Sharks and other fish with flexible skeletons have toothlike scales that feel rough to the touch.

◄▽▲▽◄◄▽▲▽◄

SWIMMING

Most fish use their tails to move themselves through the water. They use their fins to steer and remain steady.

Top and bottom fins help a fish swim upright. Side fins allow it to change direction quickly and easily.

◄▽▲▽◄◄▽▲▽◄▽

REPRODUCTION

Nearly all fish lay eggs. Some lay millions at a time. The ocean sunfish lays the most eggs: three hundred million. But only a few escape being eaten by predators.

Fish usually lay their eggs and swim away. The seahorse, however, is one of the few fish that cares for its young. Female seahorses lay their eggs in pouches in the bellies of males, who look after the eggs until they hatch.

LOOK UP: Adaptation, Biology, Camouflage, Coral Reef

Flight

FLIGHT REQUIRES THAT AN OBJECT OVERCOME THE PULL OF THE EARTH'S GRAVITY. TO FLY, A MACHINE SUCH AS AN AIRPLANE MUST PRODUCE A FORCE, OR LIFT, GREATER THAN ITS OWN WEIGHT.

LIGHTER-THAN-AIR FLIGHT

Hot-air balloons are an example of lighter-than-air flying machines. They float in the air just as wood floats in water.

The balloon's burner heats the air inside the balloon. As the air expands, some of it gets pushed outside the balloon. Although the amount of space taken up by the balloon has not changed, there are now fewer air molecules inside it. As a result, the air inside the balloon becomes lighter than the air outside it and the balloon floats upward.

When a hot-air balloon's burner is shut off, the air inside the balloon cools down and contracts, allowing more air molecules to rush in and fill the space. The additional weight of these molecules causes the balloon to fall.

HEAVIER-THAN-AIR FLIGHT

Heavier-than-air machines fly by producing a force that is stronger than the force of gravity. The most common heavier-than-air flying machine is the airplane. The most important feature of the airplane is the wing. Its shape is what allows the airplane to fly.

Airplane wings are rounded on top and flat on the bottom. Because of the way they are shaped, the air flowing on top of the wings

When the burner is on, the air inside the balloon heats and the balloon rises. When the burner is turned off, the air cools and the balloon descends.

has to travel farther than the air flowing underneath them. Because air flows together, the air flowing on top of the wings, which has farther to go, must travel faster to keep up.

When air travels faster, it tends to stretch out and become less dense. As a plane travels faster on takeoff, the air flowing on top of its wings stretches thinner and thinner. This lowers the pressure above the wings, which causes the wings to move upward.

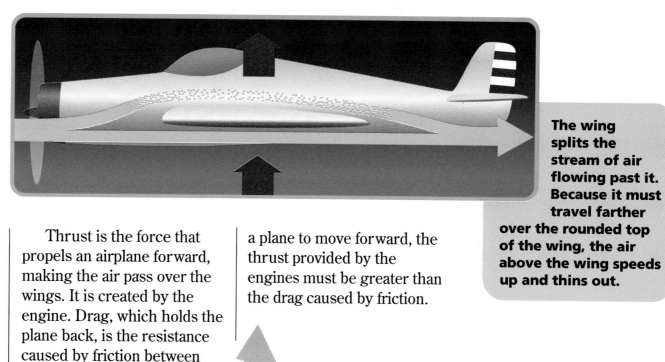

The wing splits the stream of air flowing past it. Because it must travel farther over the rounded top of the wing, the air above the wing speeds up and thins out.

LIFT
The upward force created by air moving rapidly over the wings is called lift. The force of lift must be greater than a plane's weight for that plane to take off.

Thrust is the force that propels an airplane forward, making the air pass over the wings. It is created by the engine. Drag, which holds the plane back, is the resistance caused by friction between the plane and the air. For a plane to move forward, the thrust provided by the engines must be greater than the drag caused by friction.

Lift

Drag

Thrust

Weight

Flowers

Petals

Stigma

Stamen

Ovary

The brightly colored petals and sweet scents of flowers attract bees and other insects looking for food, or nectar. Bees turn this nectar into honey.

FLOWERS MAKE THE SEEDS FROM WHICH NEW PLANTS GROW.

FLOWERING PLANTS ARE the single largest group in the plant kingdom, with about 250,000 different species. Roses, poppies, and lilies are all flowering plants. But so are grasses and many trees.

REPRODUCTION

Flowering plants usually reproduce by seed. In order for flowers to make seeds, they must first be pollinated.

The male parts of the flower are the stamens. They make and store pollen, which contains the male cells of the plant. The female parts of the flower are the stigmas, which receive the pollen, and the ovaries, which contain the unfertilized eggs.

During pollination, the male cells in the pollen fertilize the female egg cells. Some flowering plants contain both male and female parts. Others contain one or the other.

POLLINATION

Although wind spreads the pollen of some flowering plants, many more need insects to pollinate them. When bees visit one flower, pollen from ripe stamens rubs off on their bodies. As they move to another flower, they carry the pollen along with them.

As bees visit different flowers, their bodies carry pollen from the stamens of one plant to the sticky stigmas of another. From there, the male cells in the pollen travel through tubes to the plant's ovaries, where they fertilize the eggs.

Food Chain

A FOOD CHAIN SHOWS HOW THE STORED ENERGY IN FOOD PASSES FROM ONE LIVING THING TO ANOTHER.

ALL THE ENERGY IN FOOD comes from the sun. Plants at the bottom of the food chain use photosynthesis to turn sunlight into food. When an animal eats a plant, some of that energy is passed on to the animal.

Animals that eat plants are called herbivores. The next link in the food chain is the meat-eating animal, or carnivore. Carnivores get their energy by eating animals that eat plants.

PREDATOR AND PREY

Animals that hunt other animals are called predators. The animals they hunt are called prey. Lions, antelopes, and grass are all links in a simple food chain. Antelopes eat grass and lions eat antelopes.

The grass takes its energy directly from the sun. The antelopes get their energy by eating the grass, and the lions get theirs by eating the antelopes. In this example, the lions are the predators and the antelopes are the prey.

If grass in one region dies because of a drought, the antelopes there will move to another region to find a fresh supply of grass. When the antelopes move, so do the lions, because they are joined to the antelopes by the FOOD CHAIN.

FOOD WEB

In every ecosystem, food chains are always overlapping. For instance, lions also eat baboons and baboons eat both plants and smaller animals. Food chains that interlock are called food webs.

LOOK UP: Animals, Ecology, Plants

Forest

FORESTS ARE
HABITATS IN WHICH
TREES SHADE THE
EARTH FROM THE SUN.

◀▽▲▽◀▲▽▲▷◀▽

TREES ARE THE MOST
important living things in
forests because they provide
food and shelter for the
animals that live there.

◀▽▲▽◀▲▽▲▷◀▽

LAYERS

From the ground up, forests
have four different layers of
vegetation. On the forest floor,
which is the most shaded
part, dead leaves and twigs
form the litter layer.

Worms and fungi help
decompose the litter layer,
which enriches the soil. The
litter layer also includes living
plants, such as mosses and
lichens, that need little light
and thrive in damp conditions.

The next layer up is the
herb layer, which includes
leafy flowering plants and
ferns that grow where
sunlight filters through the
trees. The shrub layer, which
grows above the herb layer,
includes larger bushes,
shrubs, and young trees.

The top layer of the forest
is called the canopy. Most
woodland animals live either
on the forest floor or in the
canopy.

◀▽▲▽◀▲▽▲▷◀▽

TYPES

Forests are named for the
most common trees found in
them. Deciduous forests are
dominated by trees, such as
elms and maples, that lose
their leaves in the fall. In
coniferous forests, the
dominant
trees are
conifers, such as
pines and spruces, that keep
their leaves, or needles,
all year long.

In a deciduous
forest, the seasons
set the pace of life.
New leaves in the
spring attract
insects, which eat
the leaves. These
insects, in turn, attract
birds, which eat the insects.

In the winter, when the
trees have stopped producing
food, many forest animals
hibernate or migrate to a
warmer climate. Coniferous
forests grow farther north
than deciduous ones because
they can tolerate longer,
colder winters.

1 • OAK
The oak tree makes its own
food through photosynthesis. It
also provides food for insects, birds,
and small mammals, which eat
its bark, leaves, acorns, and
wood.

2 • HAIRY WOODPECKER
During the summer, hairy
woodpeckers probe cracks in tree
bark looking for insects to eat.
When the insects disappear
during the winter, the
woodpeckers eat seeds.

3 • LONG-EARED OWL
During the day, long-eared
owls roost in trees, their brown
plumage camouflaging them. At
twilight, they begin to hunt
mice, fish, frogs, and
insects.

4 • WOLVERINE
Although less than two feet tall, wolverines are strong and fearless carnivores, or meat-eaters. They live in northern forests where their thick fur coats protect them from the cold.

5 • CARIBOU
Caribou, also called reindeer, winter in coniferous forests. They scrape away snow beneath trees to feed on the lichen growing there.

6 • GRAY SQUIRREL
During the fall, gray squirrels bury acorns for their winter food supply. The acorns that they do not find again often sprout into new trees.

7 • CROSSBILL
Crossbills use their curved beaks to pry open pinecones and pick out the seeds.

Fossils

TRACE FOSSILS show animal tracks. No part of the animal remains, but marks preserved by ancient mud show what its footprints looked like.

FOSSILS ARE THE REMAINS OF ANCIENT ORGANISMS PRESERVED IN ROCK.

FORMATION

Fossil formation begins when a living thing dies and is buried in sand or mud. If its remains lie undisturbed for thousands of years, it may become a fossil.

During the time the dead organism lies buried, the sand or mud around it is compressed into sedimentary rock. Meanwhile, durable minerals take the place and shape of the decaying remains.

TYPES

The most common fossils are those of sea creatures, because ocean sediment is an ideal place for fossils to form. However, many land plants and animals have also been preserved. Scientists have found fossils of leaves, tree trunks, bones, teeth, eggs, skin, and even droppings.

Most land animals decay too quickly to become fossils, but some have been fossilized because they were quickly buried during a sandstorm or became stuck in a tar pit.

INDEX FOSSIL

Paleontologists use common animal and plant fossils, called index fossils, to date unknown fossils. The best index fossils to use are those of creatures that lived for a short period of time, geologically speaking. Fossils of sea creatures called ammonoids are among the most common index fossils. Between 250 million and 65 million years ago, new kinds of ammonoids evolved very quickly and became extinct nearly as fast. The presence of a particular ammonoid species in or near a fossil can date that fossil to a particular geological period.

In Arizona's Petrified Forest National Park, there are fossilized tree trunks two hundred million years old.

PALEONTOLOGY

The study of prehistoric life is called paleontology. Paleontologists study fossils to learn more about life on the earth during earlier geological periods, because fossils are records of that life.

Fossils also tell paleontologists something about what the earth's climate was like in the distant past. For example, more recent fossils supply information about the last ice age.

Fossils can also reveal information about the earth's geography millions of years ago. Fossils of sea creatures found in mountain ranges, for example, suggest that those rocks were once underwater.

DATING FOSSILS

Paleontologists can approximate when a plant or an animal lived by dating the layer of sedimentary rock in which its fossil is found. Sedimentary rock forms one layer at a time, each layer forming on top of an older one.

If a fish fossil is found in a layer of rock beneath another layer that contains a mammal fossil, paleontologists assume that the fish lived before the mammal. This is called comparative dating.

Comparative dating cannot measure in years how long ago an animal lived. To determine that, paleontologists use radioactive dating, which is a technique also used by geologists.

Paleontologists know that radioactivity decreases over time. Therefore, by measuring the radioactivity remaining in a fossilized rock, they can estimate when that rock and its fossil were formed.

CAST FOSSILS • Among the most common fossils are trilobites, which dominated the seas during the Cambrian period 570 million years ago. Because their hard shells decayed slowly, they left molds in the ocean sediment like the molds artists make using plaster. Over time, minerals filled these molds, creating the cast fossils that exist today.

Fossils are found most often in sedimentary rock, but some insect remains are found in the fossilized resin of ancient trees. These insects became trapped in sticky sap that has hardened over time into AMBER.

LOOK UP: Dinosaurs, Geology, Radioactivity, Rocks

Fruit and Seeds

FRUITS PROTECT AND NOURISH THE SEEDS OF FLOWERING PLANTS AS THEY DEVELOP.

◄▽▲▽◄◄▽▲▽◄◄▽

FRUITS CAN BE SOFT, juicy, and sweet like pineapples and peaches. Or they can be hard like acorns and pecans. They can have many seeds like bananas and apples or one seed like cherries and avocados.

According to botanists, peas and green beans are fruits because they contain seeds. So are nuts. And so are tomatoes, cucumbers, and squash. Sweet-tasting fruits are generally called fruits, while nonsweet fruits are often called vegetables.

◄▽▲▽◄◄▽▲▽◄◄▽

DEVELOPMENT

When a flower is pollinated, male cells in the pollen fertilize eggs in the flower's ovaries. Each ovary then grows into a fruit around its fertilized eggs.

Fruits are bitter until their seeds mature. This stops animals from eating them before they are ripe.

◄▽▲▽◄◄▽▲▽◄◄▽

FRUIT CYCLE

When fleshy fruits become ripe, their stems loosen and they fall to the ground where animals can eat them. The animals digest the fleshy parts but not the hard seeds inside. Instead, these seeds travel through the animal's digestive system and pass out as waste.

If no animal eats the fruit, it rots. In either case, the seeds eventually reach the soil, where they can sprout and root. The young plants they produce are called seedlings.

When seedlings grow into mature plants, they produce flowers. When these flowers are pollinated, they produce fruit and seeds of their own— and the cycle begins again.

Most fruits are good to eat because they contain nourishment for the seeds inside them.

LOOK UP: Flowers, Life Cycles, Plants, Trees

Galaxies

The bright streak in this time-lapse photograph of the Milky Way is a satellite passing overhead.

GALAXIES ARE COLLECTIONS OF STARS.

THE SUN IS ONE STAR in the galaxy we call the Milky Way. Before the twentieth century, astronomers believed that the Milky Way was the only galaxy in the universe.

In 1924, however, Edwin Hubble proved that there were other galaxies. Astronomers now estimate that the universe contains about one hundred billion galaxies.

FORMATION
The first galaxies began to take shape several hundred million years after the big bang. They formed out of huge spinning clouds of gas.

At first, atoms came together by chance. Then their combined gravity pulled in more matter. Finally, enough matter came together to form stars.

Galaxies take a number of different shapes. The Milky Way is a spiral galaxy. Its arms are constantly spinning around its disk-shaped center.

MILKY WAY
All the stars you can see at night belong to the Milky Way galaxy, which is one hundred thousand light years across. It takes the Sun about 230 million years to make a complete circle around the center of the galaxy.

In the galactic center, where the stars are crowded closely together, there is no night. Even when one side of a planet faces away from its sun, the nearby stars shine so brightly that nighttime seems like day.

Spiral Galaxy

Sun

The Sun is located in one of the Milky Way's arms, about thirty thousand light years from the center.

LOOK UP: Astronomy, Atoms and Molecules, Gravity, Matter, Stars, Universe

Genetics

GENETICS IS THE STUDY OF HOW LIVING THINGS PASS ON TRAITS FROM ONE GENERATION TO ANOTHER.

The way parental genes combine determines how a child will look. The girl on the left seems to have inherited her physical appearance from her mother (shown as a child at right). Parental genes also determine how your body grows.

TRAITS

Traits are physical characteristics. Eye color, hair color, height, and weight are all traits.

Parents pass on many traits to their children. These traits are carried by genetic information stored in the parents' sex cells.

Sex cells are unusual because they contain only half the genetic information usually stored in a cell. However, when sperm and egg cells join together during reproduction, they combine their genetic codes to create a new, complete set. In this way, the child they produce inherits some traits from the father and others from the mother.

DNA molecules are called chromosomes. Each chromosome has the shape of a twisted ladder, called a double helix. The different parts of the chromosome that determine traits are called genes.
All living things have DNA in their cells, but different species have different DNA arrangements. Some have only ten chromosomes. Others have more than one thousand. Humans have forty-six chromosomes.

DNA

The genetic code of each cell is contained in a chemical called DNA for short. Its full name is deoxyribonucleic acid. DNA is the map according to which cells grow.

Children often look like their parents because their cells contain some of each parent's DNA. However, the DNA is different for each sperm or egg cell so a child never looks exactly like its mother or father—or even its sisters and brothers.

Geography

GEOGRAPHY IS THE STUDY OF THE SURFACE OF THE EARTH AND THE LIFE ON IT.

CARTOGRAPHY, OR mapmaking, is especially important to geographers, because geographical information is often presented in the form of maps.

MAPS

Different kinds of maps are used to present different kinds of information. Road maps show the location of roads and highways. Contour maps show the heights of hills and the depths of valleys. Weather maps show weather patterns and help meteorologists forecast the weather.

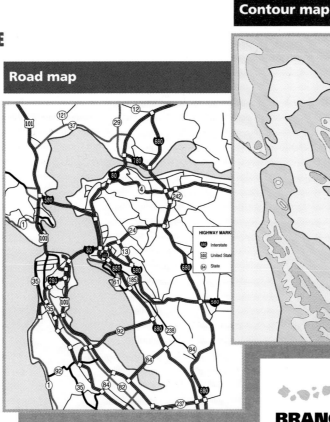

Road map

HIGHWAY MARK
- Interstate
- United State
- State

Contour map

Weather map

55
55
57
59
60
L

Some maps show very small areas, such as the center of a town or the floor plan of a house. Other maps show much larger areas: a continent, the world, or even the solar system.

BRANCHES

Geographers who study landforms, such as lakes and mountains, are called physical geographers. Because physical geographers also study how these landforms were made, their field is closely related to geology.

Biogeographers study the populations of plants and animals that live among these landforms, especially *where* they live. A map made by a biogeographer might show where a rare animal, such as the gray wolf, has been seen.

Human geography is the study of people who live in a particular area. This branch of geography overlaps economic and political studies.

LOOK UP: Earth, Geology, Weather

Geology

Radioactive elements with long half-lives can be used to date old rocks. Uranium-238, with a half-life of 4.5 billion years, can be used to date rocks as old as the earth itself.

GEOLOGISTS PAY CLOSE attention to the rocks that make up the earth. The earth's outermost layer is called the crust.

If you could slice through the earth's crust, you would find layers of sedimentary rock stacked one on top of the other. Unless these layers have been disturbed by an earthquake or a volcano, the oldest ones should be on the bottom and the youngest ones on top.

HISTORICAL GEOLOGY

By studying each layer, geologists can learn about the different periods the earth has passed through in its history. The rocks and fossils found in each layer provide important clues.

If geologists find shellfish fossils in a layer, they know that water once covered that area. If they find coal, they know that the land was once covered by a swamp, because coal forms from the remains of swamps.

The order of the layers is very important. If a fossilized fern is found many layers below a dinosaur fossil, geologists can conclude that

PRECAMBRIAN
The Precambrian period includes the first seven-eighths of the earth's history, during which time the planet took shape and life began.

CAMBRIAN
During the Cambrian period, there was no life on land, but many fish lived in the sea, as did some animals with hard shells.

Geological Period

Date Began
(millions of years ago)

Precambrian	Cambrian	Ordovician
4,600	570	500

ferns lived on that land before dinosaurs did.

RADIOACTIVE DATING

The layers in which fossils are found tell the order of the periods in the earth's history. But the order alone does not give dates for these periods. To find out how long ago these periods occurred, geologists use radioactive dating.

When rocks and fossils are formed, they often contain radioactive elements. For example, many fossils contain radioactive carbon-14, which has a half-life of about six thousand years. That is, it takes about six thousand years for half of a mass of carbon-14 to decay. After twelve thousand years, only one-quarter of the original carbon-14 remains radioactive, and so on.

GEOLOGISTS study the rocks that make up the earth. Knowing something about what lies beneath the surface can lead to the discovery of oil, coal, precious metals, and gems.

If geologists find a fossil in which only one-quarter of the original carbon-14 is still radioactive, they know that the fossil and the rock layer in which it was found are both about twelve thousand years old.

This clock represents the geological history of the earth. Think of noon as the time when the earth began to form and midnight as the present. The Precambrian era lasted from noon until 10:31 P.M. The dinosaurs lived from 11:26 P.M. until 11:50 P.M. Modern humans did not appear until just ten seconds before midnight.

CRETACEOUS
During the Cretaceous period, dinosaurs and giant reptiles dominated life on the earth.

QUATERNARY
During the current Quaternary period, human beings and other mammals have evolved.

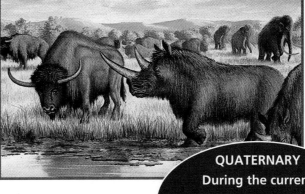

Silurian	Devonian	Carboniferous	Permian	Triassic	Jurassic	Cretaceous	Tertiary	Quaternary
	395	345	280	225	190	136	65	1.6

LOOK UP: Dinosaurs, Earth, Evolution, Fossils, Radioactivity, Rocks

Glaciers

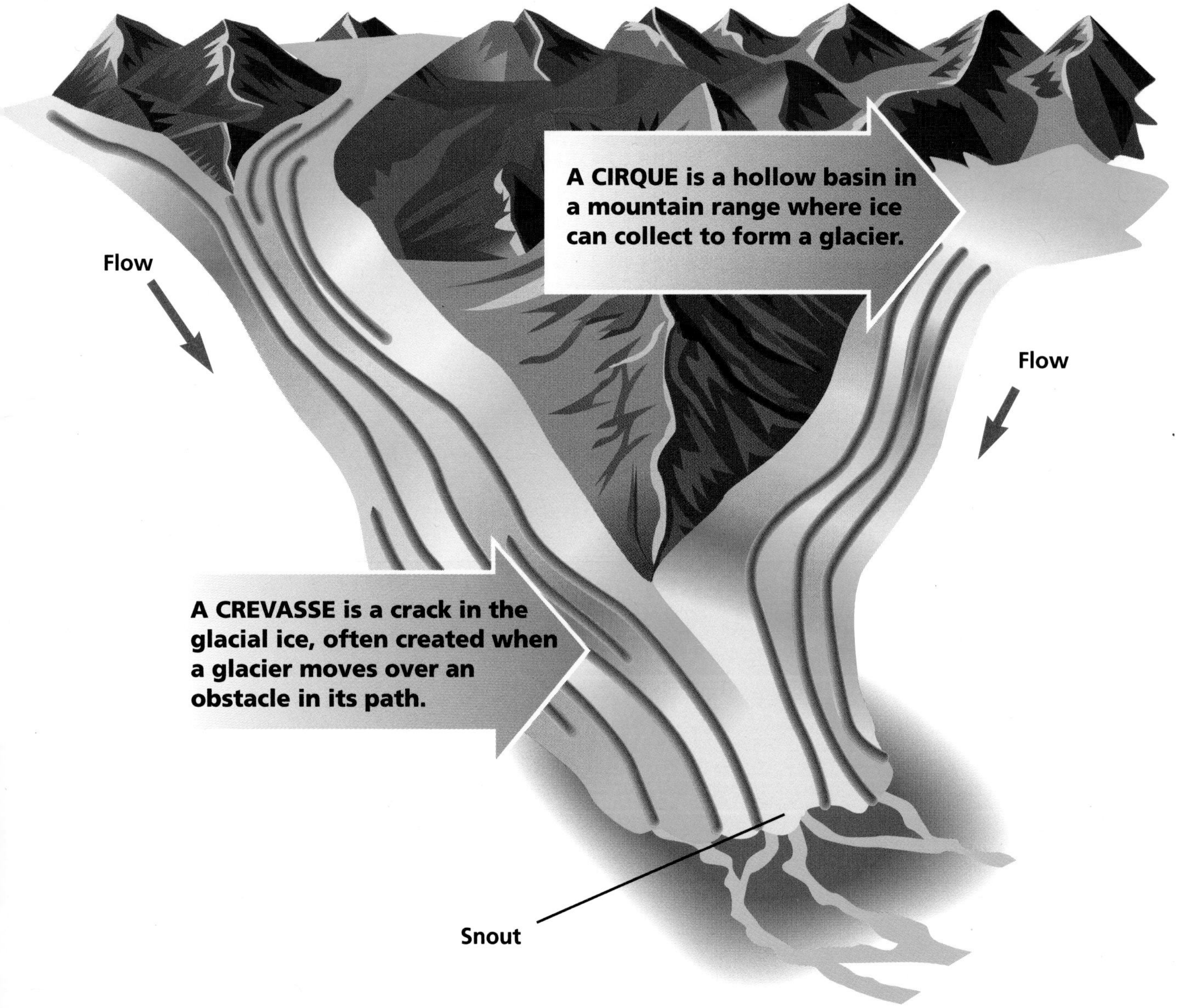

A CIRQUE is a hollow basin in a mountain range where ice can collect to form a glacier.

Flow

Flow

A CREVASSE is a crack in the glacial ice, often created when a glacier moves over an obstacle in its path.

Snout

GLACIERS ARE HUGE MASSES OF MOVING ICE.

GLACIERS TODAY COVER one-tenth of the earth's land surface, or about six million square miles. About three-quarters of the earth's fresh water is frozen in glaciers.

If all the glaciers melted, the sea level would rise high enough to put most coastal cities underwater.

FORMATION

Glaciers form in cold areas where the temperature rarely rises above 32°F, the freezing point of water. In these cold climates, which include tall mountain ranges and the earth's polar regions, the snow that falls never melts.

Over time, this snow builds up in layers like the layers of sediment at the mouth of a river. Instead of forming sedimentary rock, the layers of compacted snow form ice.

The movement of glaciers during the last ice age created many of the earth's most magnificent landforms, including YOSEMITE VALLEY in California. Glaciers also carved out the fjords of Norway, which were glacial valleys until the ice melted and seawater filled them.

Glaciers take fifty years or longer to form. They range in thickness from three hundred feet to more than thirteen thousand feet.

FLOW

As the mass of a glacier grows, its great weight pulls it slowly downhill. Glaciers can flow at many different rates, from about two feet per day to about two feet per month.

The forward edge of a glacier is called its snout. In polar regions, glaciers end where their snouts meet the sea. At this point, the motion of the sea sometimes breaks off pieces of the snout, which become floating icebergs.

Glaciers in mountain ranges farther south never reach the sea. Instead, their snouts melt as they travel downhill into the warmer air below. The freshwater produced by this melting is the source of many mountain streams.

MORAINES

As glaciers form, they pick up rocks and soil. When glaciers move, they carry this material with them, frozen in the ice.

Sometimes the rocks can be as big as houses. They help mountain glaciers carve out U-shaped valleys as they flow downhill. When the snout of one of these glaciers melts, it deposits rocks and soil in piles called moraines.

Mounds of rocks and soil that form at the front end of a glacier are called terminal moraines. Those that form along the sides of a glacier when it melts quickly are called lateral moraines.

ICE AGES

During the ice ages, glaciers covered much more of the earth's surface than they do today. Twenty thousand years ago, for example, at the end of the last ice age, one-third of the earth's surface was covered by ice.

Sometimes TERMINAL MORAINES deposited by ice-age glaciers act like dams, creating lakes in glacial valleys.

LOOK UP: Climate, Matter, Rain and Snow, Rivers, Rocks

Grassland

GRASSLANDS FORM IN REGIONS WHERE THE RAINFALL IS TOO LOW TO SUPPORT A FOREST BUT NOT LOW ENOUGH TO CREATE A DESERT.

◄▷▲▽►◄▷▲▽►◄▽

COVERING NEARLY HALF the world's land surface, grasslands get their name from the grass plants that dominate them. They receive between ten and thirty inches of rainfall per year.

Grasslands have different names in different parts of the world. South Americans call them pampas, while North Americans call them prairies. In Asia, the grasslands are known as steppes. In Africa, they are called savannas.

◄▷▲▽►◄▷▲▽►◄▽

GRASSES

Grasses are flowering plants with long, stiff stems and narrow leaves called blades. Their seeds contain foods called grains. Some of the grasses that farmers grow for their grains include wheat, oat, and rye.

Although many animals graze on them, grass plants survive because they grow from their base instead of from the tips of their stems, as other plants do. In fact, biting off the tips of a grass plant encourages it to grow more. Even if an animal eats all the stems and leaves of a grass plant, the plant can grow back as long as its ground-level shoots are not damaged.

◄▷▲▽►◄▷▲▽►◄

HERBIVORES

Grasses are the beginning of nearly every grassland food chain. Although there are not many different types of grasses, grasslands provide many different niches for herbivores, or plant-eating animals, because different animals eat different parts of the plant.

On the African savanna, for example, zebras eat the tips of grasses, while wildebeests eat the stalks. In this way, by taking advantage of different parts of the same plant, these herbivores avoid competing with one another for food.

1 • VULTURES
Vultures eat the remains of dead animals. Whenever vultures discover an injured animal, they usually circle overhead until the animal dies.

2 • CHEETAH
Vast herds of grazing animals provide plenty of food for large carnivores, such as the cheetah, which stalks its prey before running it down in a final sprint.

3 • THOMSON'S GAZELLE
Being short, the three-foot-tall Thomson's gazelle eats the part of the grass plant that grows closest to the ground.

4 • WATER HOLE
Animals come to water holes at specific times of the day in order to avoid conflicts. They also take turns drinking.

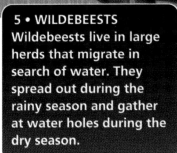

5 • WILDEBEESTS
Wildebeests live in large herds that migrate in search of water. They spread out during the rainy season and gather at water holes during the dry season.

6 • AARDVARK
Aardvarks use their sharp claws to rip open termite nests. Then they use their sticky, foot-long tongues to lick up the insects.

7 • BLACK MOUND TERMITE
African black mound termites never leave their boulder-shaped nests. Instead, they build tunnels to reach their food.

8 • ACACIA
Although grasslands do not get the rainfall necessary to support a forest, some trees, such as the acacia, do grow there singly or in very small groves.

9 • GIRAFFES
Giraffes use their long necks to feed on the leaves of trees that other animals cannot reach.

LOOK UP: Adaptation, Climate, Ecology, Food Chain, Migration, Plants

Gravity

In 1666, after watching an apple fall to the ground, British physicist SIR ISAAC NEWTON had a revolutionary idea. He thought that the force of gravity that made the apple fall might be the same force that holds the moon in its orbit.

Earth

The earth's gravity holds the moon in its orbit. The moon's gravity also affects the earth, pulling the oceans and causing the tides.

Moon

GRAVITY IS A FORCE OF ATTRACTION BETWEEN TWO OBJECTS.

GRAVITY IS THE REASON that objects fall to the ground. Without gravity, people would float off the planet and drift away into space.

EARTH'S GRAVITY
All objects produce a gravitational force. The bigger the object, the stronger the force.

The earth has such a strong gravitational force that it can hold the moon in orbit. Of course, the sun's gravitational force, which holds the earth and the other planets in orbit, is even stronger.

WEIGHT
The weight of an object on the earth is the gravitational force between it and the center of the earth.

Mars has only about one-third the gravitational force of Earth. Therefore, someone who weighs one hundred pounds on Earth would weigh only thirty-eight pounds on Mars.

Hearing

Elmo's hearing range is 20 Hz to 20,000 Hz.

HEARING IS THE SENSE PROVIDED BY YOUR EARS.

SOUND WAVES ARE vibrations in the air. Nerves in your ear translate sound waves into electrical signals that travel to your brain.

OUTER EAR

The part of your ear that you can see is called the outer ear. Its purpose is to funnel sound waves into your ear canal.

Sound waves travel through the ear canal to your eardrum. The eardrum is a thin sheet of skin covering the end of your ear canal. When sound waves hit the eardrum, they cause it to vibrate.

MIDDLE EAR

Beyond the eardrum, sounds enter the middle ear. Your middle ear has a chain of three tiny bones called the hammer, the anvil, and the stirrup because of the way they are shaped.

When the eardrum vibrates, these bones also vibrate. They carry the vibrations across your middle ear to your inner ear.

INNER EAR

Your inner ear contains a small coiled tube called the cochlea. Nerve endings in the cochlea translate vibrations caused by sound waves into electrical messages, which are sent to the brain.

There are also receptor cells in your inner ear. These cells keep track of your body's position with relation to gravity. They help you maintain your balance and tell you which way is up.

SOUND FREQUENCIES are measured in hertz (Hz). Normal human speech is about 1,000 Hz. Many animals can hear a wider range of frequencies than humans can. Dogs, which have a hearing range of 15 Hz to 50,000 Hz, can hear high-pitched whistles that humans cannot.

THE INNER EAR is located inside your skull, behind and a little below your eyeball.

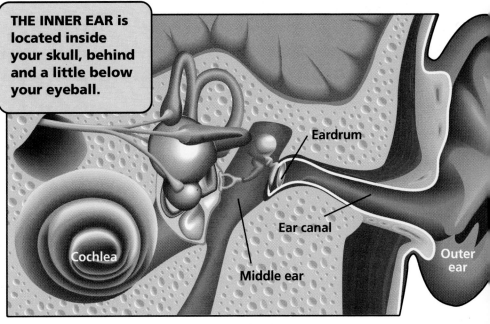

Eardrum

Ear canal

Cochlea

Middle ear

Outer ear

LOOK UP: Brain, Gravity, Senses, Sound

Heart and Blood

BLOOD contains many tiny cells floating in a watery liquid called plasma. Plasma carries digested food particles to your cells. Your blood is about half plasma. The rest is red blood cells, which carry oxygen, and white blood cells, which kill germs entering your body.

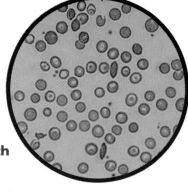

THE HEART IS THE ORGAN THAT PUMPS BLOOD THROUGH YOUR BODY.

YOUR CIRCULATORY system carries blood throughout your body. Blood carries food and oxygen to your cells. It also carries away waste.

BLOOD VESSELS
Blood travels in a system of tubes called vessels. Blood vessels form a network throughout your body.

When blood travels away from your heart, it moves in blood vessels called arteries. As they spread out, arteries divide, getting smaller and smaller. The smallest blood vessels are called capillaries.

CAPILLARIES
In the capillaries, blood drops off food and oxygen and picks up waste from the cells. Capillaries then join together to form larger and larger blood vessels.

The largest of these are called veins. Veins take the blood back to your heart.

HEART
Blood returning from your cells enters the right side of your heart. There, the right ventricle, or chamber, pumps the blood to your lungs, where it can release carbon dioxide waste and absorb more oxygen.

From your lungs, the blood returns to the left side of your heart, where the left ventricle pumps it to the rest of your body.

If you touch your neck or wrist, you can feel your pulse. Each beat indicates a contraction of your left ventricle.

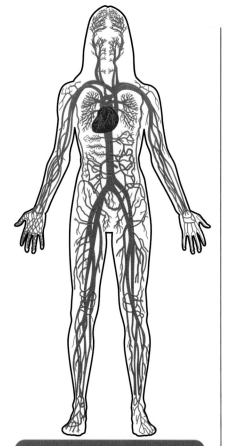

Blood that contains oxygen looks bright red. Blood that has dropped off oxygen and picked up carbon dioxide waste looks much darker.

Right atrium

Left atrium

Left ventricle

Right ventricle

Hibernation

Hibernation is a sleeping state that some animals enter to survive the winter.

◁▽△▽◁▷△▽◁▷◁▽

Most animals have difficulty finding food during the coldest winter months. Some migrate to warmer regions, where food is more plentiful. Others endure the winter by hibernating.

Animals hibernate in safe places, such as caves or burrows, where they will not be disturbed. This CHIPMUNK wakes every three or four weeks while hibernating to eat some of the food it has stored in its burrow.

True hibernators slow their bodies down until they appear to be almost dead. They do this to save energy. The body temperature of an Arctic ground squirrel, for instance, drops from 100°F to just above freezing (32°F).

Although many people think they are, BEARS are not true hibernators. Their body temperatures drop very little during the winter, and they are easily awakened. Sometimes, during warm spells, they even leave their caves to hunt.

The breathing and pulse rates of hibernating animals also fall sharply. Hibernating hedgehogs breathe only once every six minutes.

◁▽△▽◁▷△▽◁▷◁▽

PURPOSE

The purpose of hibernation is to reduce an animal's need for energy and for food. Before hibernating, animals eat as much as they can. Then, while hibernating, they live off fat they have stored in their bodies.

Most true hibernators lose about forty percent of their body weight while hibernating. When the warm weather awakens them in the spring, they are usually very, very hungry.

◁▽△▽◁▷△▽◁▷◁▽

ESTIVATION

Some animals in hot, dry climates "sleep" through the summer the way northern animals hibernate during the winter. This period of inactivity brought on by heat and drought is called estivation.

Lungfish live in shallow swamps that often dry up during the summer. To survive these droughts, lungfish bury themselves in the mud, which keeps their skin moist until the rains return.

LOOK UP: Adaptation, Climate, Migration

Human Body

THE HUMAN BODY IS MADE UP OF TRILLIONS OF CELLS. THESE CELLS WORK TOGETHER TO PERFORM THE DIFFERENT TASKS THAT KEEP YOU ALIVE.

HUMAN BEINGS HAVE about two hundred different types of cells. Groups of similar cells form body tissue.

ORGANS AND SYSTEMS

Organs are body parts that perform specific functions. They are made up of two or more different kinds of tissue.

Your body's organs work together in systems. For example, your circulatory system moves blood through your body. It consists of your heart, arteries, veins, and capillaries.

BRAIN

Your brain coordinates your body's many functions, even while you are sleeping. It controls these functions through your nerve cells. Your brain and nerves together make up your nervous system.

Breathing and circulation are basic body functions. Other, more complicated functions include speaking and solving problems.

RESPIRATION

Breathing is carried out by your respiratory system, which takes in the oxygen needed by your body's cells. The respiratory system also removes from the body carbon dioxide waste produced by your cells.

The respiratory system works closely with the circulatory system to keep

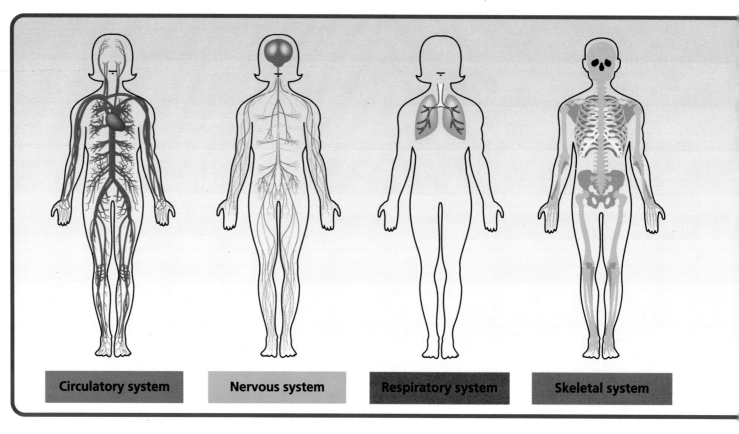

Circulatory system   **Nervous system**   **Respiratory system**   **Skeletal system**

your body alive. Your lungs breathe in the air that provides oxygen for your red blood cells. Your heart pumps these blood cells from your lungs to the different parts of your body.

SKELETON
All of your bones together make up your skeleton. The skeletal system supports your body.

Bones also protect your body's organs. Your skull holds and protects your brain. Your heart and lungs are protected by your rib cage.

MUSCLES
Muscles attached to your bones move your body. You can run, jump, and scratch your head because of muscles. Muscles also move things around inside your body. Some of these muscles, for example, move food through your digestive system.

DIGESTION
Your digestive system includes organs that process the food you eat.

During digestion, your body breaks down food into nutrients it can use. Blood cells carry nutrients as well as oxygen to your cells.

REPRODUCTION
Your reproductive system allows you to take part in creating new humans. Both mothers and fathers contribute special sex cells to their babies. These sex cells pass along important genetic information. This information determines whether a baby will be male or female, short or tall, and so on.

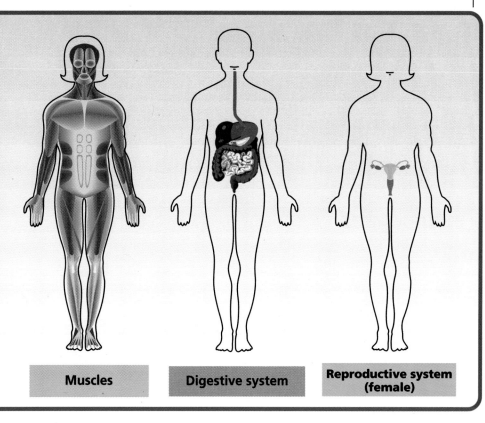

| Muscles | Digestive system | Reproductive system (female) |

Different types of cells with different jobs to do have different shapes.

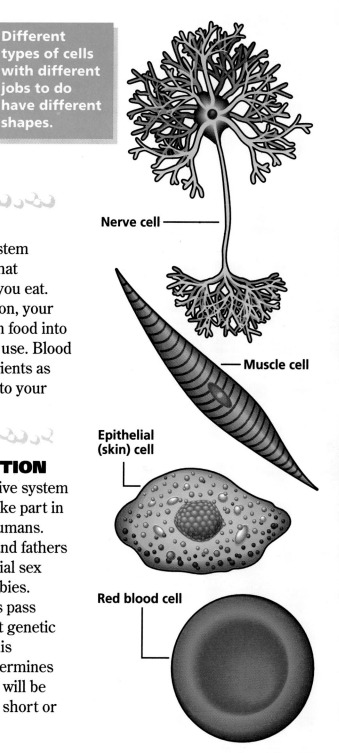

Nerve cell

Muscle cell

Epithelial (skin) cell

Red blood cell

LOOK UP: *Brain, Digestion, Heart and Blood, Lungs and Breathing, Muscles, Reproduction, Skeleton*

Hurricanes and Tornadoes

Most HURRICANES extend eight miles high into the atmosphere.

HURRICANES AND TORNADOES ARE STORMS IN WHICH HIGH-SPEED WINDS SWIRL AROUND AREAS OF LOW PRESSURE.

BOTH HURRICANES AND tornadoes cause a great deal of damage. Hurricanes affect much wider areas than tornadoes, but tornadoes have stronger winds.

HURRICANES

Hurricanes are very strong low-pressure weather systems. They start out as masses of air hovering over warm tropical water in the middle of the ocean. As time passes, they absorb moisture and heat and begin to rise.

When an air mass rises, it creates an area of low pressure beneath it. The area of low pressure at the center of a hurricane is called its eye. Winds swirl around the eye, but in the eye itself there is little or no wind.

All hurricanes begin as tropical storms. In the early stages of a hurricane, its eye is perhaps two hundred miles across and its winds are weak. The eye shrinks, however, as the winds around it pick up speed. By the time the eye has narrowed to thirty miles across, the tropical storm has become a hurricane.

Hurricanes travel along the ground at about fifteen miles per hour. They are accompanied by heavy rains.

A tornado's swirling winds are strong enough to pick up and move cars. They can also rip the roofs off houses. When these winds die down, many small objects, including animals, fall from the sky. Sometimes it really does rain frogs.

In other parts of the world, hurricanes are called cyclones or typhoons.

TORNADOES

Tornadoes are violent whirlwinds that appear suddenly during thunderstorms. They are often recognized by their funnel-shaped clouds.

The winds produced by tornadoes are the strongest found on the earth. Like hurricanes, they have a calm eye at their center.

Tornadoes usually form when a column of warm air shoots up quickly from the ground. No one is sure why this happens, but it creates an area of extremely low pressure beneath the updraft. Sometimes cool air begins to spin around this updraft, creating a tornado.

Tornado funnels can be a mile wide at their base. Wind speeds on the ground sometimes reach 370 miles per hour.

Tornadoes usually last an hour and travel about twenty miles before they disappear as quickly as they came. Tornadoes that travel over water are called waterspouts. Those that cross deserts and pick up sand are called dust devils.

The strongest winds produced by a hurricane are found just outside its calm eye. (The same is true of tornadoes.) Hurricane-force winds can reach speeds of two hundred miles per hour. They usually average about seventy-five miles per hour.

LOOK UP: Air, Atmosphere, Rain and Snow, Weather, Wind

Insects

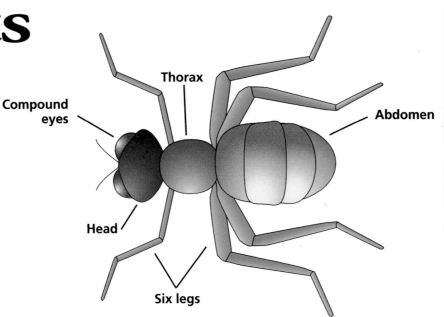

Thorax

Compound eyes

Abdomen

Head

Six legs

INSECTS ARE SMALL ANIMALS WITH SIX LEGS. THEIR BODIES ARE DIVIDED INTO THREE SECTIONS, OR SEGMENTS, AND THEY USUALLY HAVE ONE OR TWO PAIRS OF WINGS.

◄▷▲▽◄▷▲▽◄▷

INSECTS MAKE UP MORE than three-quarters of all animal species. So far, scientists have recorded nearly one million different types of insects.

Insects are invertebrates. This means that they do not have a backbone. Instead, they have a hard outer shell called an exoskeleton, which protects their soft flesh and organs.

◄▷▲▽◄▷▲▽◄▷

SEGMENTED BODY

All insect bodies are divided into three parts: the head, the thorax, and the abdomen. The head includes the insect's eyes, mouth, and antennae, or feelers.

The middle section of the body, or thorax, includes the insect's six legs and its wings. The rear section, or abdomen, holds the organs that the insect uses to digest food, breathe, mate, and lay eggs.

INSECTS have compound eyes, which means that their eyes are made up of many tiny lenses called facets. Each facet is like a small single eye. It is hard to swat flying insects because their compound eyes detect motion very well.

◄▷▲▽◄▷▲▽◄▷

METAMORPHOSIS

All insects change body form as they grow. This process is called metamorphosis.

Some insects undergo slow and simple changes in their body structures. Although baby grasshoppers lack wings and reproductive organs, they still look very much like adult grasshoppers. Because their bodies change only in minor ways, scientists call the growth process of grasshoppers incomplete metamorphosis.

Other insects experience complete metamorphosis, changing their body form entirely. Examples of complete metamorphosis are the caterpillar that changes into a butterfly and the grubworm that becomes a beetle.

HONEYBEE COLONIES can include as many as eighty thousand bees.

GROWTH

Insects grow by occasionally shedding their skin, or molting. Each time an insect molts, its new soft skin hardens quickly into a slightly larger exoskeleton.

The number of times an insect molts depends on the species. Crickets molt eight to ten times before they are fully grown.

INSECT SOCIETIES

Most insects live alone, but some live together in large groups called colonies. These social insects include ants and termites as well as some species of bees and wasps.

Social insects divide up the jobs that need to be done. In a honeybee colony, female worker bees perform most of the tasks needed to keep the hive running. They gather pollen, make the honey, build the honeycomb, care for the larvae, and repair cracks in the hive.

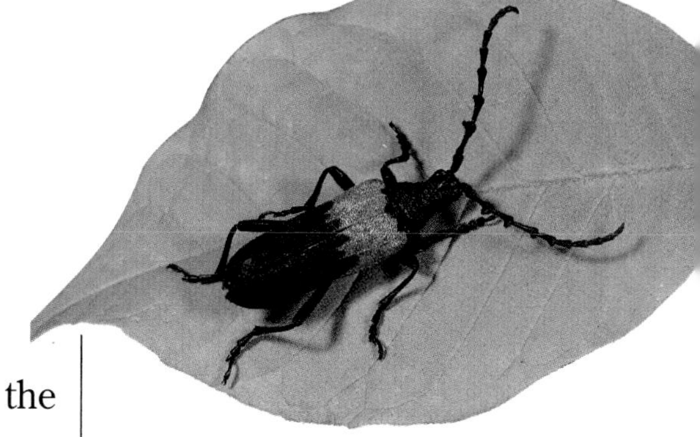

The worker bees also serve the queen bee, which lays the eggs for the entire colony—as many as two thousand a day. The only male bees in the hive are the drones, whose only job is to fertilize the queen bee's eggs.

CRABS, insects, spiders, centipedes, and millipedes are all part of the same phylum, or taxonomic group, called the arthropods. Like insects, crabs molt as they grow.

LOOK UP: Adaptation, Biology, Life Cycles, Shellfish

Lake

LAKES ARE LARGE AREAS OF WATER SURROUNDED BY LAND.

◄▼▲▼◄◄▼▲▼◄▼

LAKES PROVIDE A habitat for some species of plants and animals that are found nowhere else. Although there are saltwater lakes, freshwater lakes are more common.

◄▼▲▼◄◄▼▲▼◄▼

FOOD

Lake plants live both in the water and around its edge. They provide food for many lake animals.

Most lake food chains begin with tiny floating organisms, such as algae. Insects feed on these algae, and then fish feed on those insects.

◄▼▲▼◄◄▼▲▼◄▼

FORMATION

Most lakes are formed when rain and river water fills hollows in the ground. Lakes are usually fed by rivers or mountain springs. Falling leaves and dead plants decay to form a rich mud on the bottom of lakes, where worms and snails live.

Large lakes are home to many different kinds of plant and animal life. The ways these creatures relate to one another have often developed over hundreds of years.

◄▼▲▼◄◄▼▲▼◄▼

LIFE CYCLE

Lakes do not last forever. Some fill in. Deposits called silt build up on the bottom and sides of lakes, making them more and more shallow.

Then plants take over, creating a marsh, or wetland.

Wetlands are formed wherever water collects. They are usually found at the edges of lakes, alongside rivers, and especially in river deltas. Wetlands cover six percent of the world's total land surface.

◄▼▲▼◄◄▼▲

PONDS

Like lakes, ponds are bodies of water, but they are smaller and more shallow. Because they have less water, their ecosystems are less stable. This is because they can dry up during the summer or freeze completely during the winter.

1 • CATTAILS have underwater roots. Their stems can grow as tall as eight feet. Like other plants along the water's edge, cattails provide shelter for insects, birds, and even small mammals.

2 • MALLARD DUCK Mallards use their bills to dabble, or explore, shallow water. Sometimes they tip over to look for the plants, insects, and worms that they eat.

3 • RIVER OTTERS are mammals that live in lakes and streams. They use their webbed feet to help them swim and their tails to help them steer.

4 • NORTHERN PIKE
The northern pike is the top predator in many North American lakes. It can grow more than four feet long. It eats fish, frogs, water birds, and even small mammals.

5 • WATER LILY
The leaves and flowers of water lilies float on the surface of the water, but their long stems reach down as far as six feet to roots buried in the bottom mud.

6 • DRAGONFLY
Dragonflies are among the faster flying insects. Their larvae, called nymphs, live in the water for up to a year before metamorphosing, or changing, into winged adults.

LOOK UP: Adaptation, Ecology, Food Chain, Life Cycles, Microscopic Life

Life Cycles

LIFE CYCLES DESCRIBE THE DIFFERENT STAGES IN THE LIVES OF LIVING THINGS. THESE STAGES INCLUDE BIRTH, GROWTH, REPRODUCTION, AND DEATH.

NATURE HAS MANY cycles. Spring, summer, autumn, and winter make up the cycle of the seasons. Plants and animals have their own cycles.

Like all cycles, life cycles occur over and over again. All living things die. But plants and animals reproduce, so their species live on.

ANNUAL PLANTS

Annual plants have life cycles that correspond roughly to the seasons of the year.

During the spring, they sprout. During the summer, they grow to maturity and flower. In the fall, they release seeds from which new plants will sprout the following spring. Finally, during the winter, they die when the cold temperatures kill them.

Plants begin their lives as seeds, while animals begin their lives as eggs. Female amphibians, some fish, and some reptiles lay their eggs outside their bodies, where the males fertilize them. Almost all mammals, including humans, give birth to live young from eggs that are fertilized inside their bodies.

FOOD-TO-MINERAL CYCLE • Another important natural cycle is the food-to-mineral cycle. As the roots of a plant spread out into the soil, they take in minerals that the plant needs to grow. When an animal eats this plant, its digestive system absorbs some of the minerals in the plant tissue. The rest become waste and are returned to the soil.

BUTTERFLIES change their body form three times before reaching maturity. Each change is called a metamorphosis.

When the pupa's metamorphosis is complete, a mature butterfly emerges from the cocoon.

◄▼▲▼▲◄▲▼▲▼◄▼

SALMON

Some animals, such as the salmon, have life cycles that involve great journeys. Salmon are spawned near the sources of large rivers. When young salmon are about a year old, they swim downriver until they reach the open sea. This trip can be as long as a thousand miles.

After two or three years, the mature fish return upriver to spawn. This trip is even more difficult for the salmon. They must swim upstream and sometimes leap over waterfalls. After laying and fertilizing their eggs, the exhausted salmon die.

◄▼▲▼▲◄▲▼▲▼◄▼

INSECTS

Many insect life cycles include at least one metamorphosis, or change in body form. The butterfly, for example, has four different stages in its life cycle.

Adult butterflies lay eggs that hatch into caterpillars called larvae. Each larva then changes into a pupa, which forms a protective covering around itself called a cocoon.

SALMON always return to the rivers in which they were spawned.

LOOK UP: Amphibians, Flowers, Food Chain, Insects

Light and Color

ELECTROMAGNETIC SPECTRUM
Light is just one small part of the electromagnetic spectrum, which includes radiation of many different wavelengths. Radio waves are part of the electromagnetic spectrum. So are microwaves and X rays. But none of these can be seen by the human eye.

LIGHT IS A FORM OF ENERGY.

The water in this beaker refracts light, making the spoon appear to bend at the water line.

LIGHT IS MADE UP of tiny energy particles called photons. But these photons do not move like particles. Instead, they travel in wave form, just as sound waves do.

SPEED

Light is the fastest thing in the universe. With no resistance, it travels at a constant speed of 186,000 miles per second.

The huge distances between stars are often measured in light years. A light year is the distance that light travels in a year. The star closest to the earth, for instance, is 4.3 light years—or about 25,000,000,000,000 miles—away.

REFLECTION

Light travels in a straight line until it strikes a surface. At that point, some light will usually reflect, or bounce, off the surface.

Mirrors are excellent reflectors. A layer of silver at the back of each mirror reflects light so that you can see your reflection.

REFRACTION

Sometimes light passes through things that refract, or bend, it. For example, water bends light. That is why spoons appear to bend at the point they meet the surface of a glass of water.

The lenses in eyeglasses, cameras, and microscopes also refract light. Some lenses, such as those in magnifying glasses, make objects appear larger. Others make them appear smaller.

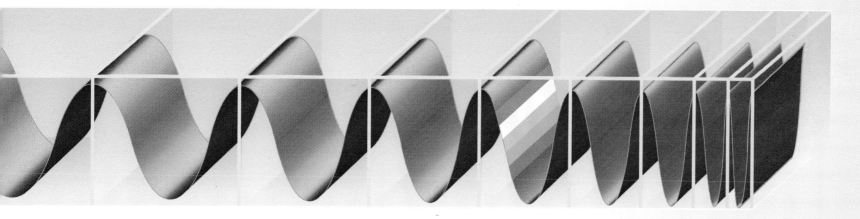

COLOR

Because light travels in waves, the length of those waves can be measured. Different wavelengths of light appear to the human eye as different colors. For example, light with a long wavelength appears red, while shorter wavelengths appear blue.

The colors that you see are all part of the visible spectrum. Light that appears white, such as sunlight, is actually made up of all the colors of the spectrum joined together.

RAINBOWS appear when drops of water in the air separate white light into the different colors of the visible spectrum.

White tents look white because they reflect all the wavelengths of visible light.

Grass looks green because it reflects green light while absorbing the other colors in white light.

Blacktop highways appear black because they absorb all the wavelengths of visible light. Black objects get very hot on sunny days because of all the light energy they absorb.

Lungs and Breathing

You can think of your trachea and lungs as an upside-down head of broccoli. The thick stem of the broccoli is your windpipe and the little green buds are your alveoli. However, your real alveoli are much, much smaller.

Nose

Mouth

Trachea

Lungs

LUNGS PASS OXYGEN FROM THE AIR TO RED BLOOD CELLS.

THE HUMAN BODY needs oxygen to live. This oxygen combines with food in the body's cells to produce energy.

Your two lungs breathe the air. They are located inside your rib cage, which protects their light, spongy tissue. Lung tissue is also elastic so that your lungs can expand as you inhale.

DIAPHRAGM
Because they do not have muscles, lungs cannot move

Bronchiole

Alveoli

At the end of each BRONCHIOLE is a cluster of ALVEOLI.

The alveoli are surrounded by CAPILLARIES. The capillaries carry blood that releases carbon dioxide and water and then absorbs oxygen.

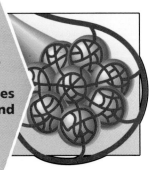

By contracting and relaxing, your **DIAPHRAGM** moves air into and out of your lungs.

People use the air they breathe to make sounds. Inside your trachea is a voice box, or larynx. Your larynx contains muscles called vocal cords. (It also makes the bump in your throat known as the Adam's apple.) When you want to speak, your brain sends messages that contract your vocal cords. The passage of air across your tightened vocal cords makes them vibrate. These vibrations make sound. Contracting your vocal cords in different ways makes different sounds.

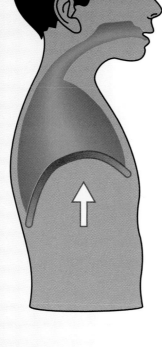

by themselves. Instead, a muscle below the lungs, called the diaphragm, helps you breathe in and out.

When your diaphragm contracts, your lungs get bigger and air flows into them. When your diaphragm relaxes, it moves upward, making your lungs smaller and pushing air out.

RESPIRATION

The parts of your body involved in breathing make up your respiratory system.

Air flows into your lungs through your trachea, or windpipe, below your throat. Near your heart, your trachea divides into right and left bronchi. Each one leads to one of your lungs.

Inside your lungs, your bronchi divide and subdivide, getting smaller and smaller. At their smallest, they are called bronchioles.

ALVEOLI

The bronchioles carry air to tiny sacs in your lungs called alveoli. A network of blood vessels surround each alveolus.

Your alveoli provide space for the exchange of gases. As your blood passes by, it releases carbon dioxide waste and absorbs oxygen.

In addition to carbon dioxide waste, your blood also drops off water. You can see this moisture when you breathe out on a cold day.

LOOK UP: *Heart and Blood, Human Body, Oxygen, Sound*

Machines

Lever

Fulcrum

By moving the FULCRUM off-center, the weight of one child can balance the weight of two.

MACHINES ARE DEVICES THAT DO WORK.

SIMPLE MACHINES MAKE work easier for people. They make heavy loads easier to lift and carry.

Mechanical machines have parts, such as wheels and pulleys, that move.

SIMPLE MACHINES

Types of simple machines include the inclined plane, the screw, the lever, the wheel and axle, and the pulley. These machines all convert, redirect, or otherwise change physical force.

Complex machines, such as the bicycle and the clock, are called compound machines because they combine two or more types of simple machine.

INCLINED PLANE

Lifting a heavy object straight up requires a lot of effort. Pushing it up an inclined plane, or ramp, is far easier, although you have to move the object a greater distance.

The loading ramp on a truck is an example of an inclined plane. Many other machines also work on this principle of exchanging effort for distance.

SCREW

The thread of a screw is a type of inclined plane. As you turn the screw, it moves forward. But the distance it moves forward is less than the distance it turns around.

This difference creates a mechanical advantage. What you lose in the distance forward, you make up in increased force.

The thread of a screw is an INCLINED PLANE wrapped around a cylinder.

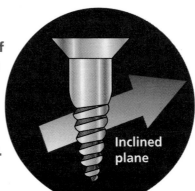

Inclined plane

LEVER

A lever is a long bar that pivots at a point called its fulcrum. A seesaw is a type of lever. So is a crowbar.

Levers are often used to move heavy objects such as boulders. Moving the fulcrum of the lever closer to the boulder reduces the amount of force needed to move it.

WHEEL AND AXLE

Wheels and axles turn force moving in a straight line into circular force. For example, a waterwheel converts the downhill force of a stream into circular motion that can turn a grindstone.

A winch does the opposite. It converts circular force (the turning of the axle crank) into force that moves in a straight line. Winches can lift objects such as the pail in a well.

PULLEY

A pulley is yet another simple machine that makes heavy loads easier to lift. A rope with a single pulley allows the lifter to pull down with the force of gravity instead of up against it.

Using more than one pulley magnifies the lifter's effort. With a double pulley system, the object being lifted moves only half the distance of the rope you pull, but the pulleys double the force of your effort.

Axle

Wheel

Pulleys

Effort

Load

Magnetism

All bars of iron have inside them millions of tiny magnets called DIPOLES.

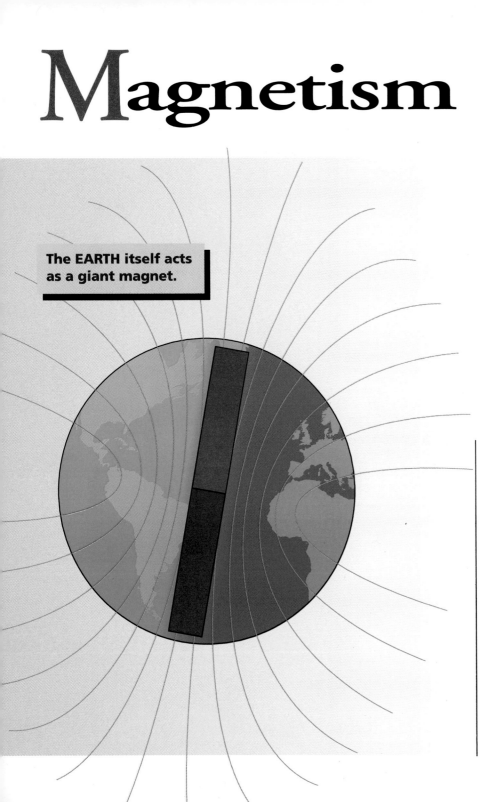

Magnetism is one of the basic forces of nature.

MAGNETS HAVE TWO ends, called poles. These poles generate magnetic fields, which are areas of force. Magnetic fields can pull objects toward one pole or the other.

EARTH AS A MAGNET
The earth itself is a magnet. Like all magnets, it has two poles. It also generates a magnetic field.

LAW OF POLES • The law of poles states that opposite poles attract (or pull together), while like poles repel (or push away).

The poles of magnets are named according to the pole of the earth, north or south, that attracts them. Magnets are strongest at their poles.

ELECTROMAGNETISM
A magnet that constantly generates a magnetic field is

N

W

S

A COMPASS works because its needle is actually a tiny magnet. The north pole of the needle always points in the direction of the earth's north pole. If navigators know which direction is north, they can also tell the direction in which they are traveling.

E

ELECTROMAGNETS show that electricity and magnetism are closely related subjects.

called a permanent magnet. Magnets that produce fields only when electricity flows through them are called electromagnets.

Electromagnets are coils of wire attached to a power source. When the power is turned on, the electric current flowing through the coils generates a magnetic field. When the power is turned off, the magnetic field disappears.

Electromagnets are useful because they can be turned on and off. There are electromagnets in televisions, telephones, computers, and many other electronic machines.

MAKING A MAGNET
An ordinary iron bar can be turned into a magnet by aligning its dipoles. This can be done by stroking the iron with an existing magnet.

Mammals

MAMMALS ARE ANIMALS THAT NURSE ON THEIR MOTHER'S MILK. MOST MAMMALS ALSO HAVE HAIR OR FUR AND ARE WARM-BLOODED.

◀▽▲▽▲◀▽▲▽▲◀▽

MAMMALS ARE NAMED after the mammary gland, or breast, that produces milk. All mammals have large, well-developed brains that make them the most intelligent animals. The class Mammalia includes three types, or subclasses, of mammals. These are the monotreme, marsupial, and placental mammals.

◀▽▲▽▲◀▽▲▽▲◀▽

MONOTREMES

Monotremes are the only mammals that lay eggs. In this way, they are like the reptiles from which the first mammals evolved.

The duck-billed platypus of Australia is the best-known monotreme. Female platypuses do not have breasts. Instead, they release milk through their skin. The milk clings to their fur, where baby platypuses lick it up.

◀▽▲▽▲◀▽▲▽▲◀▽

MARSUPIALS

Marsupials are mammals that care for their young in pouches until the babies are ready to fend for themselves. This can take weeks or months, depending on the species.

Marsupial babies are born blind and hairless with undeveloped back legs. They have front limbs, however, and sharp claws, which they use to crawl into their mother's pouch for protection. This pouch, called a marsupium, is where the mother's nipples are located.

Most people associate marsupials with Australia, where the kangaroo lives. But some marsupials live in South America, and others, such as the opossum, can be found as far north as Canada.

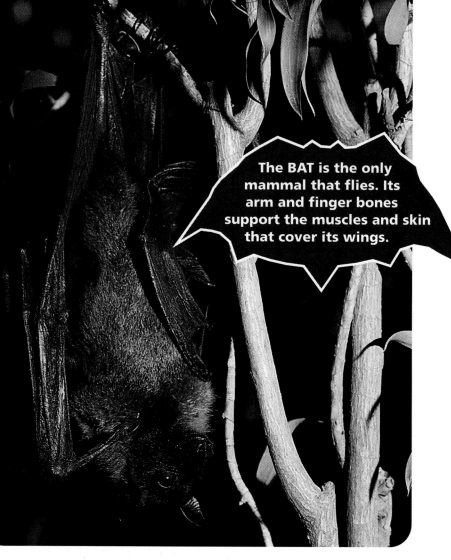

The BAT is the only mammal that flies. Its arm and finger bones support the muscles and skin that cover its wings.

All mammals are warm-blooded, which means that their body temperatures remain about the same in hot and cold weather. The normal body temperature of a GRAY WOLF is about 100.5°F.

Elmo has an average body temperature of around 98.6°F.

Rodents such as this BEAVER have four chisel-like teeth. Because their teeth never stop growing, rodents have to gnaw all the time to wear them down.

PLACENTAL MAMMALS

Of the 4,500 different species of mammals, there are three species of monotremes and about 250 species of marsupials. The rest are placental mammals, which include most of the animals familiar to humans as well as humans themselves.

Placental mammals range in size and type from the inch-long dwarf pygmy shrew, which lives in trees, to the hundred-foot-long blue whale, which lives in the ocean. Dogs, cats, cows, elephants, and lions are all placental mammals.

Young placental mammals begin development inside their mother's uterus, or womb, where they get their food through spongy tissue, called the placenta. In the placenta, the blood of the mother and her young mix together as nutrients are passed to each growing baby.

Rodents, such as mice and squirrels, are the most common placental mammals, numbering about 2,300 species. Bats are the next most common, with just under one thousand different species.

Primates are the order of placental mammals that includes monkeys, apes, and humans. All primates have eyes that face forward. They also have hands with thumbs for gripping.

DOLPHINS live in the water and have no fur. Yet they are still classified as mammals because they nurse their young. Whales are considered mammals for the same reason.

Young KANGAROOS, called joeys, are only an inch long at birth. For the next year, they live inside their mother's pouch, where they nurse on milk from her nipples.

LOOK UP: Adaptation, Animals, Evolution, Reproduction

Mathematics

$$F = 1.8C + 32$$

MATHEMATICS IS THE STUDY OF NUMBERS.

SCIENTISTS USE mathematics to study data from experiments. Meteorologists use it to find the average temperature for a particular day. Astronomers use it to predict when a particular comet will return.

FORMULAS

Scientists often use mathematical formulas to make common calculations. For instance, the formula

$$F = 1.8C + 32$$

converts temperatures from degrees centigrade (C) into degrees Fahrenheit (F).

According to this formula, to convert degrees centigrade into degrees Fahrenheit, you multiply by 1.8 and then add

32. So 100°C would be (100 × 1.8) + 32, or 212°F, which is correct.

SCIENTIFIC NOTATION

Because it is awkward to write large numbers with many zeros, scientists often use scientific notation. This system of number writing makes use of exponents, or powers, of ten.

$10^1 = 10$
$10^2 = 10 \times 10$, or 100
$10^3 = 10 \times 10 \times 10$, or 1,000
and so on.

In scientific notation, amounts are written as numbers between one and ten multiplied by a power of ten. For instance, a light year is 5,880,000,000,000 miles long. In scientific notation this number would be written as 5.88×10^{12}.

ALGEBRA is the branch of mathematics in which letters, called variables, stand for different numbers.

$$2 + 2 = 4$$

ARITHMETIC is the simplest branch of mathematics. Its operations are addition, subtraction, multiplication, and division.

GEOMETRY is the branch of mathematics that involves shapes. Five thousand years ago, the ancient Egyptians used geometry to build great pyramids.

LOOK UP: Measurement, Scientific Method, Temperature

Matter

FREEZING: LIQUID TO SOLID **CONDENSATION: GAS TO LIQUID**

MELTING: SOLID TO LIQUID **EVAPORATION: LIQUID TO GAS**

MATTER IS ANYTHING THAT TAKES UP SPACE AND HAS WEIGHT.

MATTER INCLUDES ALL the atoms in living and nonliving things.

STATES OF MATTER

Matter usually has three states. It can be either a solid, a liquid, or a gas.

At low temperatures, most matter is solid. At higher temperatures, solids melt into liquids. At even higher temperatures, liquids evaporate into gases.

The temperature at which matter changes its state varies from one substance to another. However, all matter

SOLID • The molecules in a solid are tightly packed. They cannot move around easily.

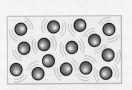

LIQUID • The molecules in a liquid slide past one another.

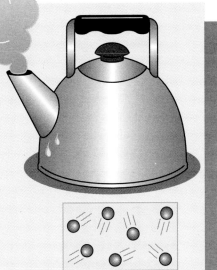

GAS • The molecules in a gas are only loosely held together. They move about freely at high speeds.

changes state when the temperature changes enough.

MELTING POINT

The temperature at which a substance changes from a solid to a liquid is its melting point.

Melting points vary. Solid water, or ice, melts at 32°F, while iron melts at 2,795°F.

BOILING POINT

When a liquid heats up to a certain temperature, bubbles

of gas form in it and rise to the surface. This temperature is the liquid's boiling point.

Different liquids have different boiling points. The boiling point of water is 212°F, while liquid oxygen boils at -297°F.

LOOK UP: Atoms and Molecules, Chemistry, Measurement, Temperature

Measurement

In ancient times, the area an ox could plow in a single day was called an acre. The size of an acre depended on the strength of the ox. Today, an acre is measured as 4,840 square yards. (A square yard is an area one yard long and one yard wide.)

Elmo's mass on the earth is 110 kilograms, and his weight is 50 pounds.

Elmo's mass in space is still 110 kilograms, but he feels weightless.

MEASUREMENTS DESCRIBE AMOUNTS.

ANCIENT UNITS

In the ancient world, people often used the lengths of different body parts as units of measure. For example, the ancient Egyptians used the cubit, which was the length of a person's arm from the tip of the middle finger to the elbow.

Cubits and other body-part measurements varied with the person who measured them. A large woman's cubit, for example, was longer than a cubit measured on a small girl.

FIXED SYSTEMS

Fixed systems produce the same measurements no matter who does the measuring. Around 1790, the French invented the metric system based on the meter (for length), the gram (for mass), and the second (for time).

In the United States, most people use the imperial system, which measures amounts in inches, pounds, and seconds. Today, scientists all over the world use a fixed system based on the metric system.

MASS AND WEIGHT
Mass measures the amount of matter in an object. An object's mass is the same in space and on the earth. An object's weight depends on the pull of gravity. As an object moves farther away from the earth, the pull of gravity weakens and the object weighs less and less.

Instrument makers have to label their measuring tools very carefully so that scientists can make accurate readings.

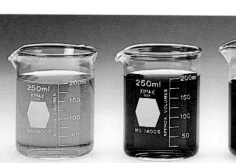

LOOK UP: Gravity, Scientific Method

Metals

IRON ORES contain iron oxides, which are mineral compounds of iron and oxygen.

METALS ARE ELEMENTS THAT CONDUCT HEAT AND ELECTRICITY WELL. MANY METALS ARE ALSO EASY TO SHAPE.

ALL METALS ARE SOLID at room temperature—except for mercury, which is a liquid. Metals generally have high melting and boiling points. For example, iron melts at 2,795°F.

Most of the known metals, such as aluminum and uranium, can be found in the earth's crust. But few are found as pure metals. Instead, they are more often found in mineral form.

SMELTING

Minerals that contain metals are called ores. Smelting is the process by which a metal is separated from the other parts of the ore.

When iron ores are smelted, they are first crushed and then loaded into blast furnaces, where they are heated until they melt. Once the iron ore melts, the heavier, pure iron sinks to the bottom of the furnace, while the other parts of the ore, called slag, float to the top.

Because copper is ductile, it can be easily drawn into wire. COPPER WIRE conducts electricity well.

PROPERTIES

Most metals are malleable, which means they can be hammered into sheets. They are also ductile, which means they can be stretched without breaking. Gold, silver, and copper are among the most malleable and ductile metals.

Metals have these properties because the patterns of their atoms can be rearranged. This is particularly true when metals are heated, as by a blacksmith.

Adding carbon to STEEL makes it stronger.

ALLOYS

When two or more pure metals are mixed together, they form an alloy. Alloys can also be formed by combining metals and nonmetals. Common alloys include brass (copper and zinc) and steel (iron and carbon).

LOOK UP: Atoms and Molecules, Chemistry, Earth, Electricity, Matter

Microscopic Life

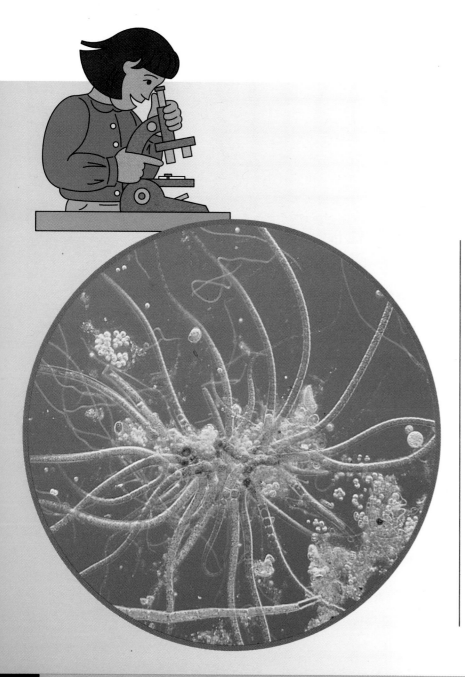

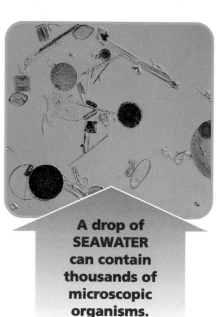

A drop of SEAWATER can contain thousands of microscopic organisms.

MICROSCOPIC LIFE INCLUDES MONERANS, PROTISTS, AND OTHER ORGANISMS TOO SMALL TO BE SEEN BY THE UNAIDED EYE.

THERE ARE TINY creatures everywhere too small to be seen without a microscope. They float in the air, live in the water, cover plants and animals, and even live inside humans. These microscopic forms of life are called microbes.

Larger animals are made up of many different kinds of cells. Each type of cell does a different job. The differences in their cells allow larger animals to do many things. But most microbes have only one cell, so they lead very simple lives.

PROTOZOA

The most common single-celled creatures belong to the kingdom Protista. Some protists, such as green algae, live the way plants do, producing their own food. Others, called protozoa, live as animals, hunting and eating their microscopic prey.

Like animal and plant cells, protist cells are made up of a nucleus surrounded by jellylike material called the protoplasm. The nucleus controls the cell's activities, including eating and reproducing.

AMOEBA

The best-known protozoan is the amoeba. Amoebas are so small that they have to be magnified one thousand times before the human eye can see them.

Like most microbes, amoebas thrive in warm, dark, wet places. They live in water, have no fixed shape, and feed by surrounding their prey.

Amoebas reproduce by splitting in two. First the nucleus splits and separates, then the protoplasm follows. This process is called fission.

BACTERIA

Bacteria are another important form of microscopic life. Bacteria are the most common living things on earth. Like protists, they are neither plants nor animals. They belong to the kingdom Monera.

Bacteria are even smaller and simpler than protists. Their single cells do not even have a nucleus.

Some bacteria reproduce by division every twenty minutes, so they spread very quickly. A single cell of BREAD MOLD can produce millions more cells in just a few hours. Although a single mold cell is too small to be seen, large colonies of mold cells are a common sight.

Bacteria interact with other living things in many different ways. Some bacteria are harmful to humans, such as those that spread disease.

The germs that cause tetanus and cholera are both types of bacteria. So are the microbes that cause milk to turn sour and bread to go moldy. People refrigerate foods to keep bacteria from spoiling them.

Other bacteria can be helpful. One example of useful bacteria is yeast, which makes bread rise. Bacteria that live in the soil play a useful role, too. They break down animal waste, returning minerals to the soil.

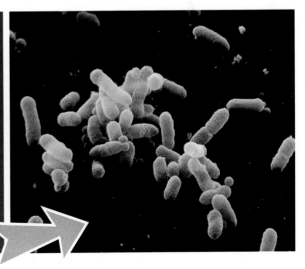

The AMOEBA's body is so thin that you can see through it.

Nucleus

Protoplasm

Bits of food are digested in small pouches called FOOD VACUOLES.

The skin around the amoeba's single cell is called its MEMBRANE.

Bacteria are one thousand times smaller than the typical animal cell. They can be seen only with an electron microscope. These INFLUENZA BACTERIA have been magnified more than four thousand times.

LOOK UP: Biology, Food Chain, Soil

Migration

MIGRATIONS ARE REGULAR SEASONAL JOURNEYS THAT ANIMALS MAKE TO FIND FOOD, SHELTER, AND A SAFE PLACE TO RAISE THEIR YOUNG.

◄▽▲◄◄▽▲▽▲◄▽

MANY DIFFERENT TYPES of animals migrate. Most migratory species are birds, but insects, fish, and mammals also migrate to winter and summer homes.

Many animals migrate to avoid harsh winter weather. Once spring comes, they travel back again.

Some swallows spend their summers feeding in Europe. Then, as winter approaches and the food supply dwindles, they fly south to Africa.

Humpback whales also migrate, but not for food, which is plentiful in the Arctic where they live. Instead, they migrate south during the breeding season because their young need warmer waters in which to grow. Later, when the baby humpbacks are strong enough to survive the icy waters, the whales return to the Arctic.

The animal that migrates the greatest distance is the ARCTIC TERN. Every year, this sixteen-inch bird flies a round trip of twenty-two thousand miles between the Arctic Circle in the north and Antarctica in the south.

◄▽▲◄◄▽▲▽▲◄▽

FINDING THEIR WAY

Migrating animals follow the same routes year after year. They use landmarks such as mountains, lakes, and rivers to find their way. Some animals have magnetic compasses inside them that guide them. Others use different senses.

Sea turtles taste the water to locate their breeding grounds in the Atlantic Ocean. Salmon use their sense of smell to guide them from feeding grounds in the ocean to the rivers where they will lay their eggs.

CARIBOU seldom stray from their migration route, even to avoid hungry wolves.

LOOK UP: Adaptation, Climate

Moon

The craters that cover much of the MOON'S surface were formed billions of years ago by large meteorites. Similar craters were also formed on Earth, but these have been eroded away by the weather. Because the Moon has no atmosphere, and therefore no weather, its craters remain.

THE MOON IS A NATURAL SATELLITE OF EARTH. IT ORBITS EARTH JUST AS EARTH ORBITS THE SUN.

THE MOON IS THE brightest object in the night sky as seen from Earth. Often it can be seen during the day as well.

Like a planet, the Moon produces no light of its own. Instead, it reflects the light of the Sun.

Except for Mercury and Venus, all the planets in our solar system have moons. Saturn has the most discovered moons—eighteen.

FORMATION

According to one theory, the Moon formed during the last stage of Earth's formation when a large interplanetary body struck Earth and knocked a chunk of the planet into space.

Although the Moon contains many of the same chemical compounds found on Earth, its smaller size has caused it to develop differently. Because the Moon has only one percent of Earth's mass, it also has much less gravity.

There is not enough gravity on the Moon to hold an atmosphere. As a result, the Moon has no air, no water, and no life. There is nothing on the Moon but rocks, dust, and a few items left behind by astronauts.

EXPLORATION

The first successful lunar probe, the Soviet Union's Luna 2, reached the Moon in 1959. During the 1960s, NASA's Apollo program sent several missions of astronauts to the Moon.

In 1968, the crew of Apollo 8 successfully entered lunar orbit for the first time. On July 20, 1969, two Apollo 11 astronauts became the first human beings to walk on the Moon.

SURFACE GRAVITY • Because the Moon has less gravity than Earth, astronauts on the Moon weigh less than people on Earth and can jump much higher.

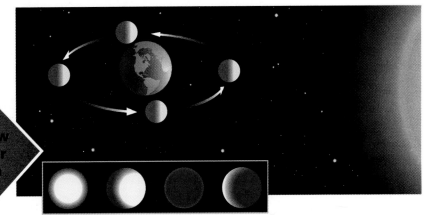

The LUNAR MONTH, which is 29.5 Earth days long, lasts from one new moon to the next. During one lunar month, the Moon passes through a complete cycle of its phases.

LOOK UP: Gravity, Planets, Satellites, Solar System, Space Flight

Motion

MOTION IS A CHANGE IN POSITION.

THE RATE AT WHICH AN object moves is called its speed. Speed in a particular direction is called velocity. Scientists calculate velocity by measuring the distance an object travels over time.

Sometimes the velocity of an object changes—for example, when cars go faster on highways. This change in velocity is called acceleration.

NEWTON'S LAWS

Isaac Newton began the modern science of physics in 1687 when he published his three laws of motion.

Newton's first law states that, unless it is pushed or pulled, an object at rest will stay at rest and a moving object will continue moving in a straight line at a constant speed.

Newton's second law states that when a force pushes or pulls an object, that object will move, accelerate, or change direction accordingly.

Newton's third law states that every force (or action) produces an equal and opposite reaction.

VIBRATION Not every kind of motion is straight ahead. Vibration is motion in a back-and-forth pattern. The swing of a pendulum, for example, is one type of vibration.

FRICTION • Friction is created when two objects, such as a brake and a bicycle wheel, move against each other.

LOOK UP: Energy, Gravity, Physics, Rockets

Mountains

MOUNTAINS ARE LANDFORMS THAT RISE HIGH ABOVE THE SURROUNDING TERRAIN.

THERE ARE MOUNTAINS both on land and under the ocean. Many mountains are still growing taller. Others are slowly wearing away.

FORMATION

When tectonic plates slide past each other, the pressure that builds up between them often causes earthquakes. When two plates collide, mountain ranges are formed.

Where the two plates meet, the earth's crust bunches up in huge folds that can reach several miles high. Depending on the way the rocky crust folds and breaks, mountains can take a number of different shapes.

AGE

Because tectonic plates move so slowly, mountains take millions of years to form. Young ones, such as the Alps in Europe, have high, jagged peaks and deep valleys.

The Appalachian mountains in the eastern United States are much older. Over time, they have been rounded down and worn away by erosion.

SNOW LINE
Beyond the snow line, temperatures never rise above 32°F (even during the summer) and the snow never melts.

ALPINE MEADOW
Below the snow line, low-lying plants grow in alpine meadows.

TIMBER LINE
Below the timber line, mountain weather is mild enough for trees to grow.

LOOK UP: Continental Drift, Earthquakes, Oceans and Seas

Muscles

MUSCLE IS THE TYPE OF TISSUE THAT MOVES YOUR BODY.

MUSCLES MOVE YOUR body by contracting, or making themselves tighter and shorter. They can pull or relax, but they cannot push.

Most muscles work in pairs to create movement. A muscle on one side of a bone pulls it in one direction, then a muscle on the other side pulls it in the opposite direction.

GOOSE BUMPS occur when the smooth muscles attached to your body hairs contract. Each muscle's contraction pulls up a single hair, creating a small bump.

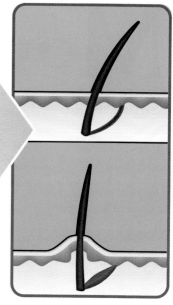

Two skeletal muscles in your upper arm work together to move your elbow. Your BICEPS muscle on the inside of your arm contracts to bend your elbow. Your TRICEPS muscle on the outside of your arm contracts to straighten your arm. As one muscle contracts, the other relaxes.

Biceps

Triceps

TYPES

There are three types of muscle in your body: smooth muscle, cardiac muscle, and skeletal muscle. Smooth muscles carry out the work of your body's organs. For example, smooth muscles move food through your digestive system. Cardiac muscle is found only in the heart. Cardiac muscle cells pump blood through your body.

SKELETAL MUSCLE

The third type, skeletal muscle, works with your bones to move your body around. Skeletal muscles are tied to your bones with connective bands called tendons.

Tendons can be very long. For example, some of the muscles that control your fingers are located between your elbow and your wrist. When these muscles contract, they pull on tendons. Those tendons in turn act like puppet strings, moving the bones in your fingers.

LOOK UP: Digestion, Heart and Blood, Human Body, Skeleton

Nutrition

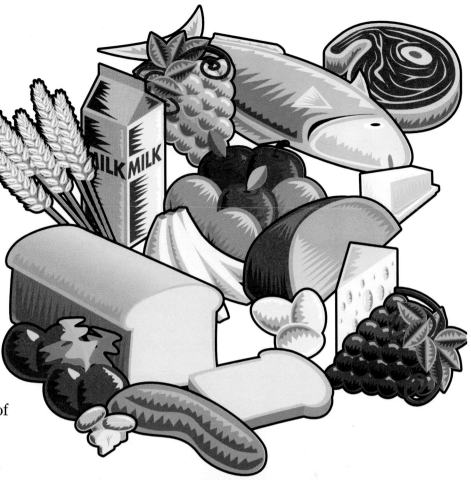

NUTRITION IS THE PROCESS BY WHICH FOOD IS SUPPLIED TO YOUR BODY'S CELLS.

YOUR DIGESTIVE SYSTEM breaks down food until it is small enough to be used by your cells. These basic units are called nutrients.

NUTRIENTS
The most common nutrients are proteins, fats, and carbohydrates. Your body uses fats and carbohydrates to give it energy. Fatty tissue also helps insulate the body from cold weather. Protein is used for growth and repair.

Vitamins and minerals are also nutrients. Your body uses them in small amounts to make chemicals that it needs.

FOOD
Some food contains more of one nutrient than another. Because your body needs a balance of nutrients, it is important to eat a variety of foods. Good nutrition means giving your body the right amount of nutrients it needs to grow and work properly.

Some foods also contain fiber. Although fiber is not digestible, it helps your body process the rest of your food more easily.

CALORIES
Calories are measures of energy. Food is often

Meat, eggs, fish, milk, nuts, and cereals are all good sources of protein. However, many of these foods also contain a lot of fat. Most nutritionists recommend that people limit the amount of fat they eat.

Fruits and vegetables provide most of the vitamins and minerals needed in your diet. Grains are one of the best sources of carbohydrates.

measured in calories. They represent the energy produced when food is used, or "burned," by your cells. A ten-year-old child needs close to 2,400 calories' worth of food each day. A stalk of celery has about five calories. A slice of cherry pie has about four hundred calories.

LOOK UP: Digestion, Energy, Fruits and Seeds, Plants

Oceans and Seas

Currents such as the GULF STREAM moderate the earth's climate. The warm water carried by the Gulf Stream makes winters in western Europe milder than in other places equally far north.

OCEANS AND SEAS ARE BODIES OF SALT WATER THAT COVER MORE THAN SEVENTY PERCENT OF THE EARTH'S SURFACE.

THE EARTH HAS FIVE oceans: the Atlantic, Antarctic, Arctic, Indian, and Pacific. All five are interconnected.

Seas are smaller bodies of salt water surrounded by land on most sides. Sometimes they are completely landlocked, but usually they are connected to oceans by passages called straits.

OCEAN WATER

Ocean water contains a number of minerals, mostly salts. These minerals come from rocks that have worn down over time. Eventually, the minerals in these rocks become dissolved in the water. Salts account for about 3.5 percent of ocean water by weight. A gallon of ocean water contains about five ounces of salt.

Some animals live deep in the ocean in areas heated by HOT-WATER VENTS. Ocean water seeps into cracks in the ocean floor, where it is heated by magma from below the earth's crust. Hot-water vents were not discovered until the 1970s.

OCEAN FLOOR

The ocean floor has many of the same physical features found on land, including mountain ranges, valleys, and plains. Some ocean islands are merely the peaks of undersea volcanic mountains.

The ocean floor also contains trenches. The deepest of these is the Mariana Trench in the North Pacific, which extends 36,201 feet below the ocean's surface. In contrast, the Grand Canyon is only about 5,300 feet from top to bottom.

OCEAN LIFE

Ocean ecosystems support a great variety of life. Microscopic plankton are the beginning of most ocean food chains.

WAVES
Waves are caused by wind blowing over the ocean. Although the wave peaks move forward, the water itself merely moves up and down. In the same way, fans in football stadiums create "waves" when they stand up and sit down one after another.

Because sunlight cannot penetrate more than a few hundred feet of ocean water, most plankton live near the surface. As a result, most fish also live in shallow water, usually within six hundred feet of the surface. Animals that live in deeper water depend on food that drifts down from above.

TIDES
High tide and low tide are the names given to the regular rise and fall of the water level along an ocean coastline. Tides are caused by the gravitational pull of the sun and the moon.

These gravitational forces pull the oceans one way and then the other as the earth and the moon move through space. The moon has a much greater effect on the tides than the sun, which sometimes works with the pull of the moon and sometimes against it.

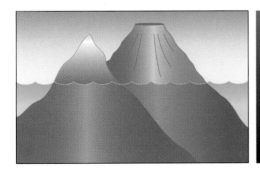

The tallest undersea mountain is Mauna Kea in Hawaii. Measured from the ocean floor, Mauna Kea is thirty-two thousand feet tall, or three thousand feet taller than Mount Everest. However, only 13,796 feet of its height is above sea level.

CURRENTS
Currents are riverlike bands of warm or cool water that flow through the oceans. They are caused by wind patterns, differences in water temperature, and the earth's rotation.

The Gulf Stream off the coast of North America travels about five miles per hour. This current carries warm water from the Caribbean all the way up to the North Atlantic and across to Europe.

LOOK UP: Climate, Continental Drift, Food Chain, Gravity, Microscopic Life, Moon

Oil

OIL FORMED FROM THE REMAINS OF PLANTS AND ANIMALS THAT LIVED IN THE SEA HUNDREDS OF MILLIONS OF YEARS AGO.

CRUDE OIL, ALSO CALLED petroleum, can be made into heating oil, gasoline, and kerosene. It can also be made into synthetic rubber, fertilizers, and even polyester. These and other chemicals made from petroleum are called petrochemicals.

FORMATION

Oil began to form during the Precambrian period six hundred million years ago when ancient sea creatures died and their bodies sank to the ocean floor. The remains of these plants and animals were buried in the mud.

As the mud slowly turned into sedimentary rock, bacteria began to break down the plant and animal remains into oil and natural gas. Because oil is lighter than water, it floats upward in groundwater.

EXPLORATION

Sometimes oil rises all the way through porous rock to the surface. Usually, however, it is trapped by layers of impermeable rock. Under these "cap rocks," drops of oil gather, forming pools called reservoirs.

Oil reservoirs are found under the ocean floor and beneath land that was once covered by an ocean. Oil companies often hire geologists to find rock formations that are likely to contain buried reservoirs of oil. Geological engineers usually explore these rock layers by drilling test wells into them.

Oil rigs are used to drill into rock layers where oil may be hidden.

In shallow water, OIL RIGS rest on the sea floor. In deeper water, their huge floating legs are tied to the bottom with cables.

Impermeable rock

Natural gas

Oil

Water

Porous rock

LOOK UP: Coal, Density, Geology, Microscopic Life, Rocks

Oxygen

OXYGEN IS THE MOST PLENTIFUL ELEMENT IN THE EARTH'S CRUST.

OXYGEN GAS MAKES UP one-fifth of the air you breathe. Oxygen is also found in many solid and liquid substances. For example, water contains oxygen.

Nearly all living things need oxygen to survive. Your body needs the oxygen in your blood to turn the food you eat into energy.

OZONE

Most oxygen gas exists in molecules made up of two oxygen atoms.

In the earth's upper atmosphere, however, energy from the sun causes a different kind of oxygen molecule to form. These molecules, called ozone, each have three oxygen atoms.

BURNING

When something burns, it combines with oxygen in the air. When wood burns, carbon in the wood combines with oxygen in the air to form carbon dioxide.

FIRE is produced when something burns. To make fire, you need heat, oxygen, and a fuel. Striking a match creates friction, which makes heat. This heat causes the chemicals on the match head (the fuel) to combine with oxygen in the air and burn.

RUST • When iron becomes moist, it combines with oxygen in the air. Instead of burning, the iron and the oxygen form rust. Painting iron can prevent rust because the paint keeps oxygen from reaching the iron.

LOOK UP: Air, Atoms and Molecules, Chemistry, Lungs and Breathing, Ozone Layer

Ozone Layer

Scientists think the CFCs used in some aerosol sprays cause holes in the ozone layer.

THE OZONE LAYER IS PART OF THE EARTH'S ATMOSPHERE. IT PROTECTS LIFE ON THE PLANET FROM EXPOSURE TO THE SUN'S MOST HARMFUL RAYS.

THE OZONE LAYER IS fifteen miles up in the atmosphere. It filters sunlight and blocks the ultraviolet (UV) rays that can harm living things. Ozone itself is a form of oxygen.

OZONE LOSS

Scientists have become concerned about damage to the ozone layer. They have noticed holes in it near the North and South Poles. The hole above Antarctica, for example, is already three times the size of the United States and continues to grow.

The effects of ozone loss are worse in some places than in others. In Antarctica, ultraviolet rays are killing off microscopic plant life. When these plants die, the animals that feed on them could disappear, too. As a result, the polar ecosystem could become unbalanced.

CAUSES

Scientists believe that much of the damage to the ozone layer has been caused by chemicals called chlorofluorocarbons, or CFCs.

These chemicals are most commonly found in air conditioners, refrigerators, and aerosol sprays. An international treaty has been signed to ban the use of CFCs by the year 2000, but meanwhile the ozone layer keeps thinning.

The OZONE LAYER normally filters out many of the sun's harmful ultraviolet rays. However, growing holes in the ozone layer now allow some of those rays to reach the earth's surface.

LOOK UP: Atmosphere, Oxygen, Sun

Parasites

PARASITES ARE ORGANISMS THAT LIVE ON OR IN ANOTHER LIVING THING AND FEED OFF IT. THEY ARE USUALLY HARMFUL.

MANY ORGANISMS LIVE together in close partnership. When only one benefits, the partner that gains is called a parasite. The creature it feeds off is called a host.

PLANTS
The rafflesia plant, which grows in the jungles of Borneo, has no roots or stem of its own. Nor does it have many green leaves, because it has no need to produce food through photosynthesis.

> **RAFFLESIA flowers, which grow more than three feet across, are the heaviest flowers in the world. They release a powerful scent that smells like rotting meat. This scent attracts meat-eating flies, which pollinate the plants.**

Instead, rafflesia plants live parasitically. They suck all the nutrients they need from the roots of host vines.

ANIMALS
Among the most common animal parasites are ticks, mites, and fleas. These tiny parasites live by attaching

> **SYMBIOSIS • When both organisms benefit from a relationship, their partnership is called symbiosis. Clown fish, for example, live in symbiosis with sea anemones. The anemone feeds on the clown fish's leftovers, while its stinging tentacles protect the clown fish from predators.**

themselves to the skin of mammals.

Most of these creatures survive by sucking blood from their hosts. The loss of blood poses little danger to the host, but the bites themselves often spread dangerous diseases. The bacteria that cause typhus, for example, are spread by human body lice.

Other parasites, mostly worms, live inside their hosts. Tapeworms living in the intestines of sperm whales can grow up to one hundred feet long.

LOOK UP: *Adaptation, Coral Reef, Plants*

Physics

OPTICS is the study of light.

PHYSICS IS THE STUDY OF MATTER AND ENERGY AND HOW THEY INTERACT.

MATTER IS ANYTHING that takes up space and has weight.

Everything in the universe, from the tiniest particle to the largest star, is made of matter.

BRANCHES OF PHYSICS

Within the field of physics, there are different areas of study.

THERMODYNAMICS is the study of heat and how it travels.

ACOUSTICS is the study of sound.

Energy can make matter move. For example, if you throw a ball, you use energy produced by your muscles to make the ball move.

FORCE

Force is a push or pull. There are many different kinds of force.

Using a bat to hit a baseball is an example of mechanical force. The batter produces mechanical force by swinging the bat.

The ball falls back to the ground because of gravity, which is another type of force.

LOOK UP: Energy, Gravity, Light and Color, Matter, Sound

Planets

A PLANET IS A LARGE, SOLID BODY THAT CIRCLES A STAR. THE STAR'S GRAVITY KEEPS THE PLANETS THAT CIRCLE IT IN ORBIT.

THERE ARE SO MANY stars in the universe that scientists believe millions of them must have their own planets. However, the only planets now known to astronomers are those that circle the Sun in our own solar system.

The planets in our solar system were formed at the same time as the Sun. They came together out of matter left over from the Sun's birth.

PLANETARY YEAR
The length of a year on any planet is the time it takes to complete a single orbit around its sun. Different planets move at different speeds, and their orbital paths have different lengths. Therefore, planets have years of different lengths.

The farther a planet is from its sun, the slower it moves and the longer it travels to complete an orbit. As a result, the planets farthest from their suns have the longest years.

It takes Earth about 365 days to orbit the Sun. A year on Mercury, though, is only 88 Earth days long, while the Martian year is 687 Earth days long. A year on Pluto, the planet farthest from the Sun, is 248 Earth years long.

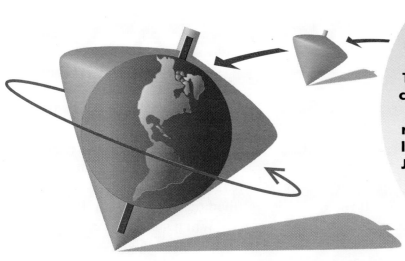

PLANETARY DAY
Planets move through space as they orbit their sun. At the same time, they also rotate, or spin, like tops. The rotation of a planet makes its sun appear to rise and set. The time that it takes a planet to rotate completely is the length of its day. Earth takes twenty-four hours to complete a rotation, so its day is twenty-four hours long. Of the planets in our solar system, Jupiter has the shortest day at less than ten hours long. Venus has the longest day, which means that it rotates the slowest. A Venutian day is 243 Earth days long.

LOOK UP: Astronomy, Gravity, Solar System, Stars, Universe

Plants

PLANTS ARE LIVING THINGS THAT USE SUNLIGHT TO MAKE FOOD.

◀▷▲▽▲◀▷▲▽▲▷◀▽

OTHER LIVING THINGS, including people, could not survive without plants. They are the main source of food on the planet. They also produce the oxygen that we breathe.

The roots of plants hold the soil in place. Without them, wind and water would sweep the soil away as easily as they do the sand on a beach.

◀▷▲▽▲◀▷▲▽▲▷◀▽

SPECIES

The study of plants is called botany. So far, botanists have identified about three hundred thousand different species of plants. Most plants have a few simple parts in common: roots, stems, flowers, and green leaves.

Plants can vary greatly in size. The smallest plants include duckweed, which measures just one-fiftieth of an inch across. Among the largest plants are sequoia trees, which grow over three hundred feet tall.

> Plants capture sunlight with a green material in their leaves called chlorophyll. During photosynthesis, the trapped solar energy in the chlorophyll causes a chemical reaction during which water and carbon dioxide change into glucose and oxygen.

◀▷▲▽▲◀▷▲▽▲▷◀▽

PHOTOSYNTHESIS

All living things need energy to live. Animals get their energy from the food they eat. Plants get their energy directly from the sun.

The process by which plants use sunlight to make their own food is called photosynthesis. All plants use photosynthesis to transform water and carbon dioxide into oxygen and a form of sugar called glucose. Glucose is the food that plants use to grow.

When animals breathe, they inhale oxygen and exhale

carbon dioxide. During photosynthesis, plants do the opposite: They take in carbon dioxide and release oxygen.

REPRODUCTION

Plants reproduce in different ways. Those that reproduce by seed are called flowering plants because seeds develop from flowers.

Flowering plants are the most common, but there are many types of nonflowering plants. Ferns and mosses, for example, reproduce by tiny spores.

After spores are released into the soil, they germinate into small plants that make eggs and sperm. Eventually, one of these sperm fertilizes an egg. From this fertilized egg, a mature plant grows.

USES

Many important products are made from plants. Rubber is made from the sap of Brazilian rubber trees. Cotton and flax plants are used to make cloth. Wood is used to make buildings, furniture, and paper. Plants from rain forests often provide the best sources for new medicines.

FERNS
Ferns have feathery leaves called fronds, and they grow well in damp, shady forests. They are descendants of the first land plants. About 260 million years ago, when the earth was covered with swamps, ferns were the most common plant life.

DIFFERENT TYPES OF PLANTS
This chart shows different kinds of plants that grow around the world.

CACTI
Cacti are flowering plants that grow in dry climates, especially in deserts. They can survive for long periods of time without rain because they store water in their fleshy stems. The sharp spines that grow on cacti protect them from thirsty animals who would otherwise eat their watery flesh.

MOSSES
Along with ferns, mosses are descendants of the oldest land plants. Because they also need shade and water, mosses are found in forests near rivers, ponds, and streams. A clump of moss is actually many tiny plants growing very closely together.

VEGETABLES
Vegetables are not a scientific class of plants. They are simply plants that people eat for food. Vegetables are usually grouped by the part of the plant that is eaten. Carrots and beets are root vegetables because their roots are eaten. Spinach and lettuce are leaf vegetables because their leaves are eaten.

GRASSES
Grasses are flowering plants with flexible stems and long, thin leaves. Because they root easily, they are often grown for food. Grasses include grains, such as wheat and rice, as well as lawn grasses. The first plant that people grew for food was an ancestor of wheat.

LOOK UP: Biology, Flowers, Food Chain, Oxygen, Soil, Trees

Pollution

POLLUTION IS THE RELEASE OF WASTE INTO THE ENVIRONMENT.

TWO HUNDRED YEARS ago, there were no cars and no nuclear reactors. When small amounts of garbage were dumped into the ocean or small amounts of coal smoke were released into the air, the earth could easily break down the pollution.

Today, factories, cars, and billions of people pollute the soil, air, and water every day. The damage that polluters do can be clearly seen in our rivers, our cities, and the air.

Pollution is often ugly, and it can also be dangerous. Pollution can make the soil unfit to farm, the water unsafe to drink, and the air bad to breathe.

ACID RAIN

When coal-burning factories release smoke into the air, a gas in the smoke called sulfur dioxide joins with water in the air to form acid rain.

When acid rain falls back to the earth, it drains into lakes and ponds, making them unfit for living things. Acid rain, which can be as strong as lemon juice, also harms birds and the trees in which they live.

CONTROLS

Environmental scientists are always working on new ways to reduce pollution and clean up the mess that it causes. New fuels, such as ethanol, burn cleaner than gasoline, and smokestack filters reduce the amount of sulfur dioxide in the air.

Laws such as the Clean Air Act and government agencies such as the Environmental Protection Agency also help control pollution. So does recycling, which can reduce the amount of a household's garbage by half.

1 • LANDFILL
The average U.S. household makes three tons of garbage per year. Most of this garbage is buried in landfills. If these landfills are not properly maintained, hazardous chemicals can leak out into the soil and groundwater.

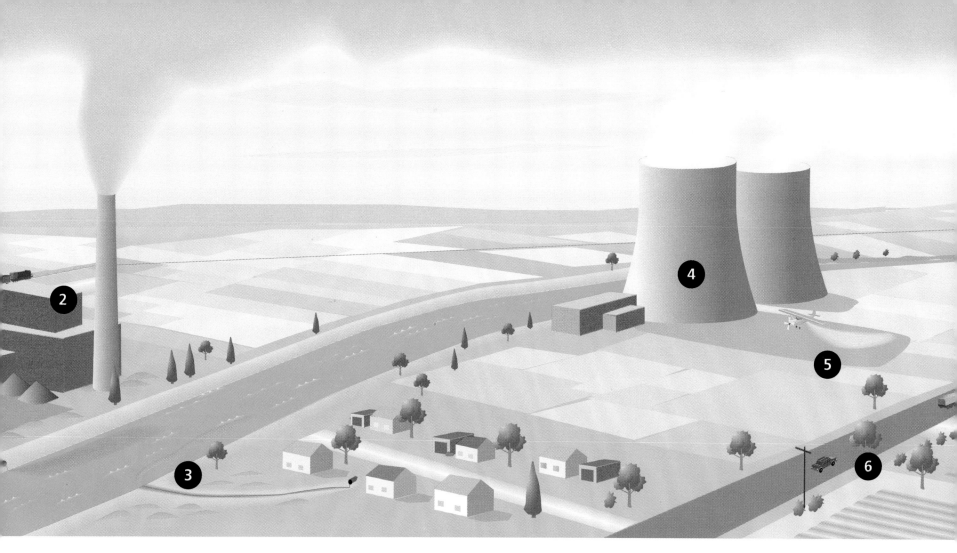

2 • FACTORIES
Many factories dump chemical wastes into the water and the soil. These chemicals can make their way into the groundwater, poisoning wells.

3 • SEWAGE
In some communities, household sewage flows untreated into rivers and oceans.

4 • NUCLEAR WASTE
Nuclear power plants make wastes that are hard to store because they stay dangerously radioactive for thousands of years.

5 • PESTICIDES
Farmers use pesticides to kill weeds and crop-eating insects. But often these poisons run off into rivers and lakes, where they kill plants and animals that live there.

6 • AUTOMOBILE EXHAUST
Car engines give off carbon monoxide and other poisonous fumes. They are a major source of air pollution.

LOOK UP: Coal, Energy, Radioactivity

Radio

RADIO IS THE TRANSMISSION AND RECEPTION OF ELECTROMAGNETIC SIGNALS WITHOUT WIRES.

RADIO WAVES ARE PART of the electromagnetic spectrum. They are similar to light waves, except they have much longer wavelengths.

Receivers pick up radio waves traveling through space. Some radio waves occur naturally. They are produced by stars, along with light and other electromagnetic rays.

MARCONI
In 1896, the Italian inventor Guglielmo Marconi patented a way to use radio waves to broadcast messages. Marconi's transmitter worked by converting electrical signals into radio waves.

These waves were then picked up by a receiver that converted them back into electrical signals. Marconi's system was called "wireless telegraphy" because it worked like a telegraph, only without wires.

AM AND FM
Radio stations today broadcast programs as Marconi did by varying, or modulating, the radio waves they produce. One way to do this is to vary the height, or amplitude, of the waves.

AM radio signals vary the height, or amplitude, of the waves.

FM radio signals vary the frequency of the waves.

Amplitude modulation is how AM radio works.

Broadcasters can also vary the frequency of the waves they transmit. (The frequency of a wave measures how often its peak-and-trough cycles repeat.) FM radio works by frequency modulation.

AM radio signals carry farther, but FM radio produces a clearer signal.

Radioactivity

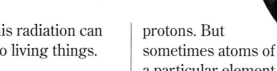

Scientists use Geiger counters to detect and measure radioactivity.

RADIOACTIVITY IS THE PROCESS BY WHICH CERTAIN ATOMS GIVE OFF ENERGY AS THEY SPLIT APART.

As RADIOACTIVE ATOMS break apart, they give off streams of high-energy particles. This radiation can be harmful to living things.

ISOTOPES

All atoms of the same element have the same number of protons. But sometimes atoms of a particular element have different numbers of neutrons.

Atoms of the same element with different numbers of neutrons are called isotopes. Their overall charge is the same, but they may behave differently. Often one of these isotopes is radioactive.

For example, normal carbon-12 atoms, which have six protons and six neutrons, are stable, but carbon-14 isotopes, with six protons and eight neutrons, are radioactive.

HALF-LIFE

The half-life of a radioactive substance is the time it takes for half its atoms to disintegrate.

For some elements, this process can be very slow. For example, it takes 4.5 billion years for one-half of a sample of uranium-238 to decay into lead-206.

Geologists use radioactive elements such as uranium-238 to date rocks and fossils. By measuring how much of the radioactive material in the rock or fossil has decayed, they can tell when it formed.

LOOK UP: Atoms and Molecules, Chemistry, Energy, Fossils, Geology

Rain and Snow

RAIN AND SNOW ARE DROPS OF WATER THAT FALL TO THE GROUND. SNOWFLAKES ARE FROZEN CRYSTALS OF WATER.

AIR NEARLY ALWAYS HAS water vapor in it. Warm air can hold more water vapor than cold air.

When warm moist air cools, the water vapor in it condenses, or turns into a liquid. When enough water turns from vapor into liquid, it collects in clouds and falls to the ground as rain or snow.

PRECIPITATION

Precipitation is the general name given to forms of water that fall from clouds. Besides rain and snow, other forms of precipitation are sleet, drizzle, and hail.

Because most clouds form high above the ground, where the air is very cold, precipitation usually starts out as snow.

TYPES

The type of precipitation that reaches the ground depends on the air temperature. If the temperature of the air at ground level is below the

SNOWFLAKES are groups of microscopic ice crystals frozen together.

THUNDERSTORMS occur during warm weather when moist air rises and cools very quickly. The ice and water droplets that form inside thunderclouds bump into each other, knocking electrons loose from the ice. The electrical charge that builds up in each cloud is released as lightning.

The lightning heats the air around it to about 54,000°F, which is more than five times hotter than the surface of the sun. This heat causes the air around the lightning to spread out faster than the speed of sound, making thunder.

HAIL
Hail forms inside tall storm clouds that reach up to six miles high. Air currents inside these clouds sometimes carry drops of rain back up into higher altitudes where they freeze again, forming hail. Often, these little balls of ice will move up and down several times, adding a new layer of ice each time, before they fall to the earth.

freezing point of water (32°F), the precipitation will remain frozen and fall as snow.

However, if the air temperature at ground level is above freezing, the snowflakes will melt and turn to raindrops. When the temperature hovers around the freezing point, sleet falls. Sleet is partially frozen rain.

WATER CYCLE
Rain and snow are both part of the water cycle. Water from the earth's lakes, rivers, and oceans is always evaporating into the air, which also absorbs the water vapor exhaled by plants and animals.

When air containing water vapor rises, it cools, and the water vapor condenses to form clouds. When enough condensed water collects in a cloud, it falls to the ground as precipitation.

Precipitation may fall on mountains or plains or even on a glacier. In any case, it eventually flows back into a body of water, where it evaporates and keeps the water cycle going.

RAINBOWS are produced when sunlight hits raindrops in the air at a certain angle. The raindrops act like prisms, separating the white sunlight into the different colors of the visible spectrum.

LOOK UP: Air, Clouds, Electricity, Hurricanes and Tornadoes, Light and Color

Rain Forest

TROPICAL RAIN FORESTS ENJOY WARM TEMPERATURES AND HEAVY RAINFALL THROUGHOUT THE YEAR.

◀▷▲▽◀◁▷▲▽▲▷◀▽

RAIN FORESTS ARE FOUND near the equator, where the sun's rays remain strong all year. Temperatures generally range between 68°F and 82°F, and rain falls in short bursts nearly every day. Although as much as 160 inches of rain can fall in a year, 70 inches is more typical.

◀▷▲▽◀◁▷▲▽▲▷◀▽

DIVERSITY
The warm, wet, sunny, and stable conditions in a rain forest are ideal for living things. As a result, rain forests support the greatest variety of life on the planet.

Although tropical rain forests take up less than ten percent of the earth's land surface, they hold more than half of the world's plant and animal species. Only coral reefs are nearly so rich.

Most of these species live in the treetop layer, called the canopy. Because the canopy receives the most sunlight, it is usually a mass of branches, leaves, fruit, and flowers.

◀▷▲▽◀◁▷▲▽▲▷◀▽

PLANTS
In rain forests, plants are always competing with one another for sunlight. Vines, for instance, use trees for support as they climb toward the light in the canopy.

Rain forest trees also support plants known as epiphytes, or "air plants," because they root on tree limbs rather than in soil. They are not parasites, however, because they take their nutrients from the air and the rain.

◀▷▲▽◀◁▷▲▽▲◁

WILDLIFE
Most rain forest animals live in the canopy, because they can find the most food there. These animals have adapted so well to living in trees that many of them never touch the ground. Some use their tails as an extra hand to grip tree branches.

1• BOA CONSTRICTOR Some boa constrictors grow up to eighteen feet long. They kill small animals by constricting, or squeezing, them until the animals can no longer breathe.

2 • BROMELIADS are plants that can hold up to two gallons of water in the funnel formed by their leaves. Snakes often lurk near bromeliads, waiting for prey that might stop by for a drink.

3 • HARPY EAGLE
Harpy eagles nest in the tallest trees. They fly over the canopy, hunting macaws, monkeys, and sloths.

4 • THREE-TOED SLOTH
Three-toed sloths use their curved claws to hang upside down from tree branches. Because they cannot walk and must pull themselves around, they rarely go down to the forest floor.

5 • TOUCAN
Toucans use their large, brightly colored beaks to frighten away other birds, especially hawks. They also use their beaks to pick fruit, which they sometimes juggle before swallowing.

6• RED-EYED TREE FROG
Rain forests are so damp that some frogs, such as the red-eyed tree frog, spend their entire lives in the trees. They lay their eggs in pools of water that form in the leaves of epiphytes.

Reproduction

REPRODUCTION IS THE PROCESS BY WHICH HUMANS CREATE NEW LIFE.

ALL LIVING THINGS create new beings, or children, like themselves. Individual creatures may die, but species live on from one generation to another because they reproduce.

Human beings reproduce sexually. Sexual reproduction means that both the male and the female contribute cells to their child. Humans produce special sex cells, called gametes, that join together to make a baby.

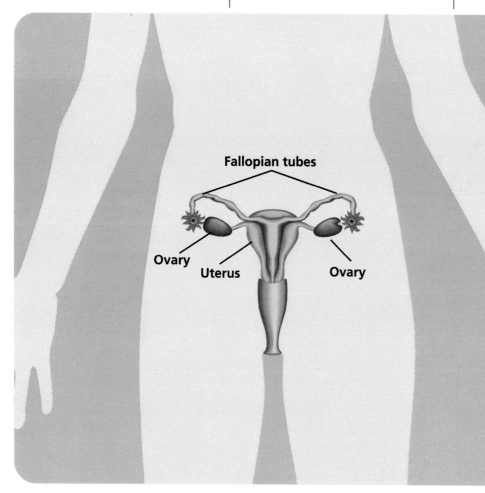

Fallopian tubes

Ovary

Uterus

Ovary

SEX CELLS

The male sex cells are called sperm cells. They are produced by male sex organs called testicles. Sperm cells leave a man's body through his penis.

Female sex cells are called egg cells. They are made in the female sex organs, called ovaries. When ovaries release egg cells, they move down the fallopian tubes toward the woman's uterus.

FERTILIZATION

Together, male and female sex cells create new offspring. When a male sperm cell finds a female egg cell, it joins with it. This process is called fertilization. Egg cells must be fertilized before they can start growing and become babies.

After fertilization, the combined egg-and-sperm cell divides to form two new cells. Then each of these new cells divides, making a total of four cells, and so on.

BABIES

By this process of cells dividing over and over again, the fertilized egg grows.

During the first eight weeks after fertilization, it is called an embryo. Once it takes on some basic human characteristics, doctors call it a fetus. Even at eight weeks old, however, the fetus is still only one inch long.

A fetus grows inside its mother's uterus, where a placenta forms. The placenta is spongy tissue that connects the growing fetus to its mother, whose blood feeds it.

Blood vessels inside the placenta allow oxygen and nutrients to move from the mother's blood to the fetus. As the fetus gets larger, the mother's uterus and belly expand. It usually takes about nine months from fertilization for a pregnant woman to give birth.

SONOGRAMS are pictures made using sound waves. Doctors use sonograms to study the condition of a fetus growing inside its mother's womb.

At the end of three months, fetuses are still just a few inches long. However, during the next six months, their weight increases more than one hundred times, and they can grow another eighteen inches in length. The fetus shown in this sonogram is six months old.

Eyes

Hand

The skin, or membrane, of the egg cell controls its fertilization. The membrane of an unfertilized egg cell will allow a single sperm cell to pass through it. After the egg is fertilized, however, its membrane becomes impenetrable. This way, only one male sex cell can fertilize each egg.

Reptiles

If a predator, such as a bird, grabs a **LIZARD** by its tail, the tail usually snaps off, allowing the lizard to escape. The lizard then grows another, shorter tail as a replacement.

REPTILES ARE COLD-BLOODED ANIMALS. THEY LIVE PRIMARILY ON LAND AND HAVE DRY, SCALY SKIN.

REPTILES WERE THE FIRST vertebrates, or animals with a backbone, to leave the water permanently. Their move onto land, which happened about 320 million years ago, was made possible by their dry,

watertight skin. This important adaptation helped prevent early reptiles from losing too much body moisture.

DINOSAURS

During the next hundred million years, reptiles evolved slowly. About 220 million years ago, a group of very large reptiles called dinosaurs appeared. The word *dinosaur* means "terrible lizard."

Dinosaurs became extinct, or died out, about sixty-five million years ago. The species that survived evolved into the reptiles that live among us today.

TYPES

There are three groups of reptiles living today: the chelonians, the squamates, and the crocodilians.

The chelonians include both turtles and tortoises, which are turtles that live entirely on land. Chelonians are unique among reptiles

because of their hard, bony shells.

Snakes and lizards together make up the squamates. They look different today, but snakes and lizards evolved from the same ancestors. Scientists who study fossils believe that snakes were once lizards that gradually lost their legs.

TURTLES, which have horn-covered jaws instead of teeth, feed on plants and small animals.

All but a few reptiles lay eggs. Most snakes and lizards lay their eggs in shady holes and leave them. ALLIGATORS AND CROCODILES, however, look after their young.

CHAMELEONS change their skin color to blend in with their surroundings. Like most lizards, they eat insects, which they catch with long, sticky tongues. A chameleon's tongue can be as long as its entire body.

SNAKES can eat animals wider than their bodies because their jaws can stretch very wide.

The crocodilians include both crocodiles and alligators, which live partly in water and partly on land. Although they look like giant lizards, crocodilians are actually more closely related to dinosaurs. You can always tell a crocodile from an alligator because the fourth tooth in a crocodile's lower jaw sticks out even when its mouth is closed.

◁▷▽▷◁▷▽▷◁▽

SKIN
Most reptiles have tough, scaly skin, which they shed as they grow. Lizards shed their skins gradually, while snakes usually shed their skins in one large piece.

Although some reptiles, such as the poisonous Gila monster, have brightly colored markings, most blend into their surroundings. This camouflage helps them sneak up on prey and avoid the attention of other predators.

◁▷▽▷◁▷▽▷◁▽

COLD-BLOODED
Reptiles are cold-blooded, so their body temperature changes according to the temperature of the surrounding air. When the weather is cold, reptiles move slowly and eat less. When the temperature warms up, they become more active.

To keep their body temperatures down, reptiles living in deserts usually take cover during the day, either in a shady place or underground. Crocodiles and alligators sometimes keep their mouths open as a way of cooling off.

A fourth group of reptiles has only one species: the TUATARA. Tuataras live on just a few tiny islands in the Pacific Ocean off the coast of New Zealand. The tuatara has remained almost unchanged since the time when dinosaurs roamed the earth.

LOOK UP: Adaptation, Biology, Camouflage, Desert, Dinosaurs, Evolution

Rivers

RIVERS ARE LARGE STREAMS OF FRESH WATER THAT FLOW INTO LAKES OR THE SEA.

THE AMOUNT OF WATER a river carries can change dramatically depending on the weather and the season. During droughts, some rivers may dry up. During very rainy periods or after unusual snowmelts, rivers can flood.

SOURCES

Rivers often begin as very small rivulets or streams fed by mountain springs and melting snow. As they run downhill, these streams join together to form larger water flows. Eventually, enough streams join together to form a river.

Rivers can also begin at the snouts of melting glaciers or below lakes that overflow.

FLOODPLAIN

As rivers flow quickly down mountainsides, they carve channels. Some of the rock particles worn away by the river fall to the bottom and form a thin layer of sediment. Others are carried along by the current.

When a river reaches an area of flatter land called a floodplain, it begins to slow down. When this happens, the river water warms and water plants begin to take root.

A floodplain is the area covered by water when a river overflows its banks. Floodplains are usually good farming land because floodwaters deposit rich river sediment over them. This sediment improves the soil.

DELTA

Most rivers eventually flow into the sea. There, they deposit whatever remains of the sediment they have collected during their journey from the mountains.

The lower end of a river, called its mouth, sometimes meets the sea in a wide area called a delta. River deltas are made up of many different streams separated by islands of accumulated sediment.

Other rivers pass into the sea through channels called estuaries, in which freshwater and seawater mingle.

1 • WATERSHED
A watershed is a ridge that divides two river systems. Depending on which side rain falls, it flows into one system or the other.

2 • CANYON
The erosion caused by rivers can change a landscape. The rushing waters of the Colorado River, for example, carved out the Grand Canyon. When river waters move slowly over soft rock, gently sloping river valleys form. When rivers run quickly through hard rock, they dig deep gorges.

3 • RAPIDS
Rapids usually occur when a river flows down a steep slope or when its channel narrows.

6 • DELTA
Sediment builds up over time to form deltas.

4 • FLOODPLAIN
Down on the floodplain, rivers often wind back and forth in lazy bends called meanders.

5 • TRIBUTARY
Streams that feed rivers are called tributaries.

LOOK UP: Glaciers, Lake, Rain and Snow, Rocks

Rockets

ROCKETS USE POWERFUL JETS OF GAS TO LAUNCH OBJECTS INTO SPACE.

DURING THE 1680S, Isaac Newton stated that for every action, there is an equal and opposite reaction. This was one of his three laws of motion.

Rockets work on this principle. By burning fuel, they create jets of exhaust gas that rush rapidly out of nozzles. The downward push of these gas jets causes an equal and opposite reaction, launching the rocket upward.

LIQUID FUEL

The first rockets were thirteenth-century Chinese fireworks that burned gunpowder. In 1926, however, American engineer Robert Goddard made an important breakthrough when he built the first liquid-fueled rocket.

Before Goddard, rockets could travel only within Earth's atmosphere because they needed oxygen to burn their fuel. But Goddard's rocket could travel in space because it carried with it chilled liquid oxygen.

SATURN V

The most powerful rocket ever built was the Saturn V. It was designed for the Apollo program, which sent the first astronauts to the Moon.

Each Saturn V rocket was 360 feet tall and weighed more than five million pounds. It carried its fuel in three separate stages. When each stage was used up, it dropped away, lessening the load.

ESCAPE VELOCITY

If you throw a ball straight up, it quickly slows down and falls back to Earth. But if you could throw that same ball with the force of a rocket, it would never come back.

The speed required to break free of a planet's gravity is called its escape velocity. Earth's escape velocity is 24,480 miles per hour. The escape velocity is the same for all objects, but it takes much more force to launch a heavy object than a light one.

Command module

Service module

Third stage

Second stage

First stage

LOOK UP: Astronomy, Gravity, Oxygen, Physics, Space Flight

Rocks

ROCKS ARE SOLID MASSES OF MINERALS THAT MAKE UP MOST OF THE EARTH'S CRUST.

ROCKS ARE CLASSIFIED BY the way they are formed. There are three types of rock: igneous, sedimentary, and metamorphic.

IGNEOUS

Magma is molten rock found deep inside the earth, where the temperature is very hot. Lava is the name given to magma that pours out of volcanoes when they erupt.

As magma cools, igneous rocks form. Many igneous rocks, such as granite, form slowly underground. Others, such as pumice, form quickly on the surface after volcanic eruptions.

SEDIMENTARY

Although igneous and other rocks are very hard, they break up over time and wear away. Wind and rain carry these rock particles into rivers and oceans, where they collect on the bottom in layers called sediment.

As new layers of sediment form, older layers underneath them become more compact. Eventually, the weight of the top layers presses the bottom layers into sedimentary rock such as sandstone (from sand) and shale (from clay).

METAMORPHIC

Metamorphic rocks form underground where heat or pressure cause changes in a rock's minerals. For example, when the weight of a mountain presses down on a layer of sedimentary shale, the shale turns into slate. Or when nearby magma heats a layer of sedimentary limestone, the limestone turns into marble.

Each of the colored specks in this piece of GRANITE represents a different mineral crystal. Most rocks contain as many as six different minerals.

Igneous rocks, such as pumice, form as magma or lava cools.

Metamorphic rocks, such as gneiss, form underground when sedimentary rocks are exposed to heat or pressure.

Sedimentary rocks, such as limestone, form in compressed layers of worn-away rock.

Satellites

SATELLITES ARE OBJECTS THAT ORBIT LARGE CELESTIAL BODIES SUCH AS PLANETS.

THE MOON IS A NATURAL satellite of Earth. There are also many satellites made by scientists orbiting Earth.

Scientific satellites perform many useful tasks. Some observe the weather. Spy satellites monitor events around the world.

Communications satellites relay television and telephone signals from one continent to another. Navigational satellites help ships and airplanes locate their positions.

OPERATION

Sunlight is a major source of power for many satellites. They use photoelectric cells, which cover their sides, to turn sunlight into electricity.

Satellites communicate with ground stations by radio. Their signals are collected by antennae called satellite dishes.

ORBIT

The path a satellite takes around Earth is called its orbit.

Satellites at different altitudes orbit Earth at different speeds. The higher a satellite's orbit, the slower its orbital speed. Satellites close to Earth orbit faster than the planet rotates.

GEOSTATIONARY ORBIT

There is one particular orbit, however, at which a satellite's speed matches the speed at which Earth turns. This orbit occurs 22,280 miles above the equator. Satellites at this altitude are said to be in geostationary orbit.

Geostationary orbits are very useful. Because satellites in geostationary orbit move at the same speed as Earth's rotation, they constantly hover over the same spot on Earth.

Satellites parked in geostationary orbit form a relay network that can transmit communications instantly around the world.

Spy satellites take elliptical orbits, which bring them very close to their targets and then very far away.

Weather satellites fly in polar orbits, which allow them to observe the entire planet as it turns.

LOOK UP: Energy, Moon, Planets, Space Flight, Weather

Scientific Method

SCIENTIFIC METHOD IS THE PROCESS BY WHICH SCIENTISTS MAKE AND TEST NEW THEORIES ABOUT HOW THE UNIVERSE WORKS.

SCIENTIFIC WORK IS usually careful and orderly. Scientists suggest possible explanations for why things are the way they are, then they test those explanations to confirm or disprove them.

OBSERVATION

Most scientists begin their study of an event by observing it carefully over a period of time. They often use measuring instruments to collect information, or data, about the event.

Scientists use this data to think up theories to explain the event. To test these theories, scientists design experiments.

EXPERIMENTATION

Experiments allow scientists to compare theories and decide which one best explains an event. Scientists should always test a new theory before deciding whether or not the theory is correct.

Once a theory has been accepted, scientists often use it to predict the results of future events. Some theories, however, can never really be proven.

Although many scientists work in laboratories, many others conduct their experiments in the field. These biologists are working in the field, marking an endangered species of bog turtle.

LOOK UP: Measurement

Seasons

SEASONS ARE PERIODS OF THE YEAR ASSOCIATED WITH PARTICULAR TEMPERATURES AND WEATHER PATTERNS.

EXCEPT NEAR THE equator, most regions of the world experience regular changes in their weather during the course of a year. During spring and summer, air temperatures rise. During autumn and winter, they fall.

EARTH'S TILT

Seasons exist because the earth is tilted on its axis in relation to its orbit. This means that one-half of the planet is always leaning closer to the sun. The sun's rays hit this half longer and more directly, producing warmer temperatures.

For half of the year, from the first day of spring in the Northern Hemisphere until the last day of summer there, the earth's tilt leans that half of the planet closer to the sun.

The sun does not set at the North Pole from the first day of spring until the last day of summer. The same is true of the South Pole during its spring and summer.

However, because the earth moves around the sun, the seasons change. During the other half of the year, the earth's tilt leans the Southern Hemisphere closer to the sun, bringing spring and summer to that region, while the Northern Hemisphere endures autumn and winter.

The tropical regions around the equator are a special case. No matter the season, the sun there is always directly overhead, so they remain warm all year long.

Sun rays that hit the earth directly warm the air more than rays that hit the earth at an angle.

Indirect rays

Direct rays

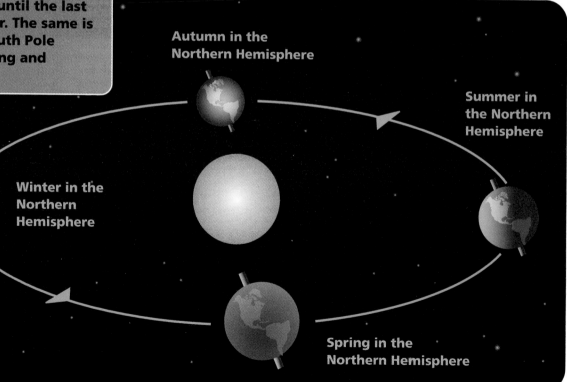

Autumn in the Northern Hemisphere

Summer in the Northern Hemisphere

Winter in the Northern Hemisphere

Spring in the Northern Hemisphere

LOOK UP: Planets, Sun

Senses

SENSES COLLECT INFORMATION FROM THE WORLD AROUND YOU.

TYPES

There are five senses: hearing, sight, smell, taste, and touch. The body has different sensory organs for each type of information.

You see because your eyes are sensitive to light. You hear because your ears are sensitive to sound. You have the sense of touch because nerve endings in your skin are sensitive to heat and pressure.

Your nose and your tongue are both sensitive to chemicals. Your nose smells chemicals floating in the air. Your tongue tastes chemicals dissolved in your food.

ANIMAL SENSES

Some animals have senses that are better than human senses. For example, dogs have sharper senses of smell and hearing, while golden eagles can see prey as small as a field mouse up to half a mile away.

Many animals—such as the RATTLESNAKE, which hunts at night—have special senses. To find their prey in the dark, rattlesnakes use special sense organs located in pits in their upper jaw. These pits sense heat given off by small mammals. They make it possible for rattlers to "see" their prey without light.

Scientists often use tools to improve their senses. Astronomers, for example, have long used telescopes to see things far away. This TELESCOPE, built by William Herschel in 1789, was considered a technological wonder of the eighteenth century.

LOOK UP: Astronomy, Hearing, Sight, Smell, Taste, Touch

Shellfish

SHELLFISH ARE ANIMALS WITH HARD, OUTER COVERINGS THAT LIVE IN WATER.

MOLLUSK SHELLS are made of minerals taken from seawater. They grow outward to protect the mollusk's soft, fleshy body.

THE TWO MAJOR GROUPS of shellfish are crustaceans and mollusks. Although their name sounds like fish and they live in the water, shellfish are not related to fish. In fact, crustaceans and mollusks are not even related to each other.

CRUSTACEANS

Insects and spiders are part of the phylum, or taxonomic group, called the arthropods. Crustaceans are also arthropods. In many ways, crustaceans are the insects of the sea.

Like insects, they grow by molting, or shedding their shells. They also have antennae, segmented bodies, and jointed legs.

Crabs, lobsters, and shrimp are all crustaceans. So are many of the countless microscopic creatures that make up ocean plankton.

MOLLUSKS

Mollusks are the second-largest group of invertebrates after the arthropods. While crustaceans molt many times during their lives, mollusks have only one shell, which grows along with them.

Scientists divide mollusks into a number of different groups. The most important ones are the gastropods, the bivalves, and the cephalopods.

GASTROPODS

Gastropods are the largest group of mollusks. They have a single spiral shell that holds a fleshy, muscular "foot." Gastropods use this foot to move around.

Most gastropods live underwater, but some are land-based. Snails, conches, and whelks are all gastropods. The slug is thought to be a gastropod that lost its shell.

BIVALVES

Clams, oysters, and scallops are typical bivalves. Bivalve shells have two parts.

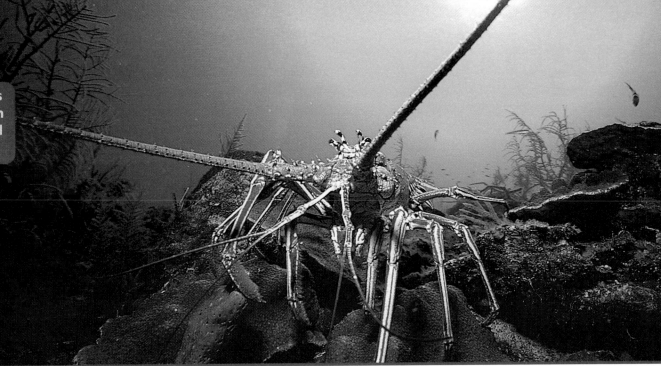

The two halves of a bivalve shell are joined by a hinge of flesh. When bivalves are threatened, strong muscles pull the halves tightly together to protect the soft flesh inside.

◄▷▲▽◄◄▷▲▽▷◄▽

CEPHALOPODS

Octopuses and squid are the best-known cephalopods. Octopuses have no shells.

Squid carry their shells inside their bodies. Still other cephalopods have shells outside their bodies.

Part of each cephalopod's foot acts like a pump, shooting out a jet of water that pushes the animal forward. The rest of the foot is divided into

Although PEARLS are rarely found in nature, Japanese experts have developed ways to inject grit into oysters to make them.

tentacles. Octopuses have eight tentacles. Squid have ten.

◄▷▲▽▲▽◄◄▷▲▽▷◄▽

PEARLS

Sometimes a piece of grit, such as a grain of sand, gets inside an oyster's shell.

Because the oyster's body is soft, the grit can be very irritating. To make the grit more bearable, the oyster coats it

When they are threatened, OCTOPUSES squirt a cloud of ink to confuse their enemies.

with a substance called nacre, or mother-of-pearl. Pearls are bits of grit that have been completely covered with nacre.

LOOK UP: Adaptation, Biology, Insects, Microscopic Life, Spiders

Sight

SIGHT IS THE SENSE PROVIDED BY YOUR EYES.

YOUR EYES COLLECT information in the form of light. Nerves in your eyes translate this light into electrical signals that travel to your brain.

PUPIL

After passing through several layers, light enters your eye through an opening called the pupil. The pupil is the dark spot in the center of your eye. The colored part of the eye around your pupil is called the iris.

Your pupils get bigger or smaller depending on how much light there is. On sunny days, your pupils become smaller to protect your eyes from receiving too much light. At night, your pupils expand to let in more light.

RETINA

Behind the pupil is the lens. The lens focuses the light entering through your pupil on the retina. This light forms an image on your retina.

The retina contains millions of light-sensitive nerve endings called rods and cones. They line the inside of your eyeball. Cones help you see colors in bright light. Rods help you see in dim light.

Rods and cones translate light into electrical nerve signals. These signals are then sent to your brain by way of the optic nerve at the back of your eyeball.

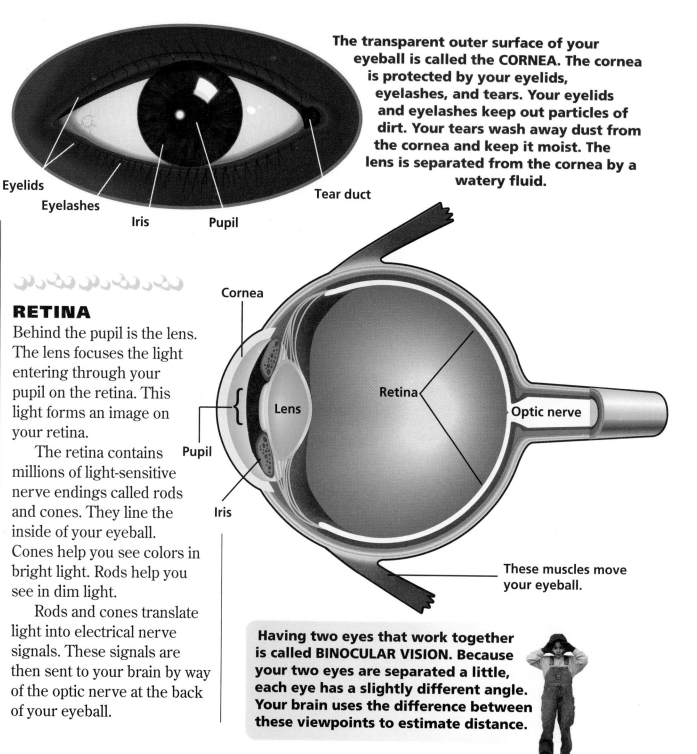

Eyelids
Eyelashes
Iris
Pupil
Tear duct

The transparent outer surface of your eyeball is called the CORNEA. The cornea is protected by your eyelids, eyelashes, and tears. Your eyelids and eyelashes keep out particles of dirt. Your tears wash away dust from the cornea and keep it moist. The lens is separated from the cornea by a watery fluid.

Cornea
Retina
Lens
Optic nerve
Pupil
Iris

These muscles move your eyeball.

Having two eyes that work together is called BINOCULAR VISION. Because your two eyes are separated a little, each eye has a slightly different angle. Your brain uses the difference between these viewpoints to estimate distance.

Skeleton

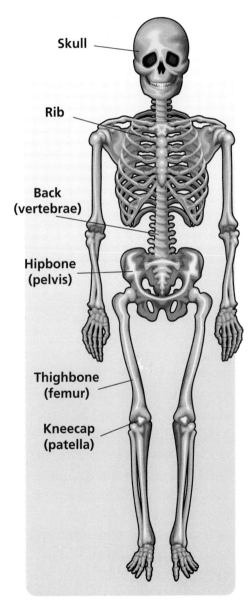

Skull

Rib

Back
(vertebrae)

Hipbone
(pelvis)

Thighbone
(femur)

Kneecap
(patella)

THE SKELETON IS THE FRAMEWORK OF BONES THAT SUPPORTS YOUR BODY.

THERE ARE ABOUT 206 bones in the body of an adult man or woman. The largest of these is the thighbone, or femur, which runs from the hip joint to the knee.

The smallest bones in your body are inside your ear. These inner-ear bones are less than one tenth of an inch long.

BONES
Bones give shape to your body and protect its fragile organs. Taken together they form your skeleton.

Because bones have living cells, they grow as you do. That is also why broken bones heal.

Bones store minerals such as calcium around their living cells. These minerals make your bones firm and hard.

Bones meet at JOINTS. These joints are held together by tough connective tissue called ligament. The smooth ends of your bones are protected by layers of cartilage. Fluid in each joint allows your bones to slide past one another.

Joints allow you to bend, turn, and twist your body. Your elbow is a hinge joint. It allows your arm to bend. Your shoulder is a ball-and-socket joint. It allows your arm to swivel. Together, these joints allow your arm to move in many directions.

CARTILAGE
When bones first form in a baby, they are mostly made of cartilage. Cartilage is a tough, flexible substance that gradually hardens into bone as you grow older.

Some cartilage, such as the cartilage at the tip of your nose, never turns to bone.

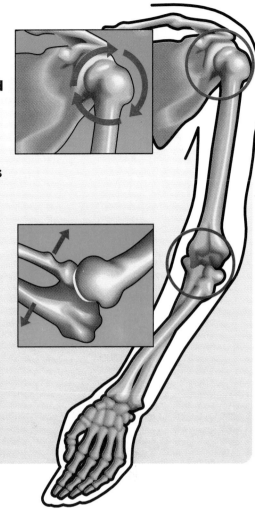

BONES AND MUSCLE
Muscles work with bones to allow you to move your body. Your muscles pull against the framework of your skeleton. Muscles are connected to your bones by strong cords called tendons.

LOOK UP: *Hearing, Human Body, Muscles*

Smell

SMELL IS THE SENSE PROVIDED BY YOUR NOSE.

YOUR NOSE DETECTS odors, which are chemicals floating in the air. It then translates these odors into electrical signals that travel to your brain.

Strong odors indicate a high concentration of chemicals. Weak odors mean there are fewer chemicals in the air.

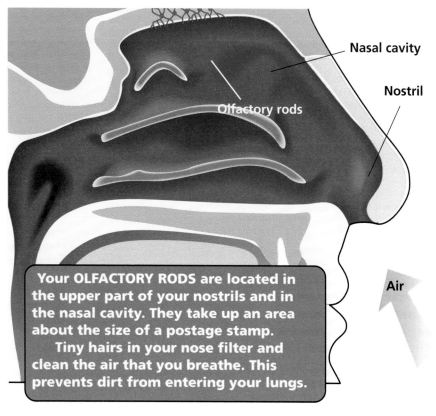

Nasal cavity

Nostril

Olfactory rods

Air

Your OLFACTORY RODS are located in the upper part of your nostrils and in the nasal cavity. They take up an area about the size of a postage stamp.

Tiny hairs in your nose filter and clean the air that you breathe. This prevents dirt from entering your lungs.

To smell something more carefully, people usually sniff the air. Sniffing brings more air into your nose—and with it, more of the odor-causing chemical.

OLFACTORY RODS

Inside your nose are nerve endings called receptors. These receptors work in the same way as the nerve endings in your skin.

The receptor cells in your skin help you touch. The receptors in your nose help you smell. Nasal receptors are also known as olfactory rods.

MUCUS

The olfactory rods in your nose are protected by a slippery substance called mucus. (When you blow your nose or sneeze, mucus comes out.)

As you breathe, the mucus inside your nose traps chemicals that cause odors. Through the mucus, these chemicals touch your olfactory rods.

When your olfactory rods are stimulated by one of these chemicals, they send a message through your nervous system to your brain. Different chemicals stimulate the olfactory rods in different ways and cause different messages to be sent. Your brain interprets these messages as smells.

Dogs have a better sense of smell than humans because their noses have many more receptor cells. POLAR BEARS also have an excellent sense of smell. They can smell a dead seal up to twelve miles away.

LOOK UP: *Brain, Human Body, Lungs and Breathing, Senses, Taste*

Soil

SOIL COVERS PARTS OF THE EARTH'S SURFACE AND HELPS PLANTS GROW.

SOIL LOOKS LIFELESS AND dull, but many soils are crawling with life. Even a small handful of dirt can contain thousands of microscopic creatures.

Worms, insects, and spiders all live in the soil. So do burrowing mammals such as moles and field mice.

COMPOSITION

Soil is a mixture of minerals and dead plant and animal matter. The minerals come from rocks that have been worn down by the weather. Soil is constantly being mixed up by rain, melting snow, the growth of plant roots, and the burrowing of animals.

Many gardeners make large piles of their grass clippings, fallen leaves, and vegetable scraps. As these piles decompose, or rot, the plant matter inside them forms a rich mixture called compost that helps plants grow.

The roots of plants dig holes that allow air to pass through the soil.

TOPSOIL • Small plants root in the topsoil, which contains most of the soil's humus.

SUBSOIL • The roots of larger plants and trees grow down into the subsoil, which is rich in minerals.

BEDROCK • Erosion breaks up the top layer of the bedrock. Cycles of freezing and thawing slowly lift these broken pieces into the subsoil.

When plants and animals die, their remains decay into a material called humus. As more plants and animals grow and die, more humus is added to the soil layer, making it thicker.

TYPES

Scientists classify soil according to the size of the rock pieces in it. The size of these pieces determines how well the soil will drain and whether humus will cling to it.

Sand and gravel, which are large grains of rock, drain very well, but they hold little humus. Silt is made of finer grains of rock that hold more humus. Clay is made of very small grains of rock that tend to stick together when wet. Clay does not drain well and may not hold much humus either.

The best soils for growing plants are loamy, which means that they have both large and small grains of rock in them. Loamy soils balance the needs plants have for good drainage, air, and plenty of humus.

LOOK UP: Microscopic Life, Plants, Rocks

Solar System

Mercury

Venus

Earth

Mars

Jupiter

The rock-and-metal planets are separated from the gas giants by a band of rocks called the ASTEROID BELT. Asteroids are rocks that orbit the Sun like small planets. The largest are more than six hundred miles across, but most are the size of a house or smaller. Many are the size of pebbles. Some astronomers believe the enormous gravity of Jupiter prevented this material from clumping together when the rest of the planets formed.

OUR SOLAR SYSTEM INCLUDES THE SUN AND THE NINE KNOWN PLANETS THAT ORBIT IT. IT ALSO INCLUDES ASTEROIDS, COMETS, PLANETARY MOONS, AND FLOATING COSMIC DUST.

OUR SOLAR SYSTEM IS shaped like a disk. All the objects in our solar system, except comets, orbit the Sun in the same direction.

The planets spin around the Sun in roughly the same level, or plane—except for Pluto, which is the planet farthest from the Sun. Our solar system is more than seven billion miles across.

PLANETS

The nine known planets in our solar system vary greatly in size, surface temperature, atmosphere, and gravity. They are usually divided into two groups: the rock-and-metal planets and the gas giants.

The rock-and-metal planets include the four planets closest to the Sun: Mercury, Venus, Earth, and Mars. The next four planets are the gas giants: Jupiter, Saturn, Uranus, and Neptune. Pluto is usually classed by itself.

The gas giants are much larger than the rock-and-metal planets. They do not have a surface on which you could stand. Instead, they are made up of layers of gases and liquids surrounding a small rocky core.

Earth is the only planet known to sustain life. It is also the only planet in our solar system with liquid water on its surface.

MARS is called the "red planet" because of the rusty iron in its soil. The Martian sky has a pinkish color because of all the red dust floating in the atmosphere. This photo was taken by the Viking 1 probe, which landed on Mars in 1976.

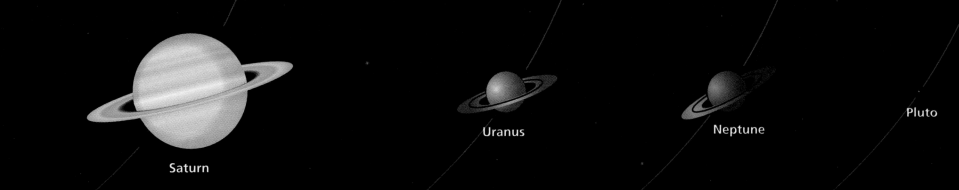

Saturn

Uranus

Neptune

Pluto

PLUTO

Pluto is so far from Earth that, even through a telescope, it looks like a bright star rather than a planet. It is the smallest planet in our solar system and the only one not yet visited by a space probe.

There are a number of curious things about Pluto, which is smaller than Earth's moon and made up of rock and ice. Astronomers have long wondered how such a small rocky planet came to be in a place so far from the other rocky planets.

This mystery has led many astronomers to question whether Pluto really is a planet at all. Some think it may have once been a moon of Neptune that broke away.

Every 248 years Pluto's unusual orbit brings it closer to the Sun than Neptune. Between the years 1979 and 1999, for example, Neptune is the planet most distant from the Sun.

PLANET X

Neptune was first observed in 1846 and Pluto in 1930. But astronomers had predicted their existence because their gravities affected the orbits of other planets.

For the same reason, some astronomers believe that there might still be an undiscovered tenth planet, called Planet X. The gravity of Pluto alone does not fully explain the orbits of Uranus and Neptune.

If Planet X does exist, it is most likely dark like Pluto and two to three times the size of Earth.

SATURN'S RINGS • Around 1655, Dutch astronomer Christian Huygens became the first person to observe the rings of Saturn through a telescope. Later astronomers, using more powerful telescopes, discovered that the rings were not solid, because stars could be seen through them. The Voyager space probes finally showed that Saturn's rings are made up of pieces of ice, rock, and dust.

Sound

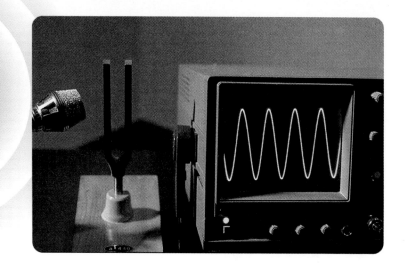

At room temperature, Elmo's voice travels at 1,125 feet (343 meters) per second.

SOUND IS A FORM OF ENERGY THAT TRAVELS IN WAVES.

OBJECTS THAT PRODUCE sound make vibrations in the air. We hear sound when these vibrations reach our ears and make our eardrums vibrate with the same pattern.

Sound travels in waves, just as light does. But unlike light, sound cannot travel in a vacuum. It needs molecules of matter to carry its energy from one place to another.

WAVE MOTION

Scientists measure sound with an instrument called an oscilloscope. Oscilloscopes display sound waves as patterns of wavy lines.

The horizontal distance between peaks in a sound wave is called the wave's frequency. The height between the peak (top) and the middle of the wave is called its amplitude.

If you use binoculars to watch a MARCHING BAND far away, you will see the cymbals crash together before you hear the sound of the crash. That is because light travels nearly one million times faster than sound.

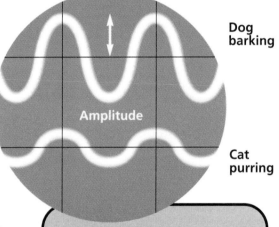

PITCH • Pitch describes how high or low a sound is. Pigs squeal at a high pitch. Cows moo at a low pitch. High-frequency sound waves have high pitches. Low-frequency sounds have low pitches.

High voice

Frequency

Deep voice

Dog barking

Amplitude

Cat purring

LOUDNESS • High-amplitude sound waves are louder than low-amplitude waves. Scientists measure loudness in units called decibels (dB). A motorcycle engine roars at close to 90 dB, while people whisper at about 30 dB.

There is no sound on the MOON because there is no air to carry the sound waves.

ECHO

Like other waves, sound waves bounce off objects in their path. Some objects reflect sound waves better than others. Materials that do not reflect sound waves well are often used for soundproofing.

Sometimes sound waves bounce wildly around a large empty room. Echoes are waves that bounce all the way back to your ears.

SPEED OF SOUND

Sound waves in the air travel at different speeds depending on the temperature, humidity, and altitude. In general, sound travels slower in cold air than it does in warm air.

Sound also travels faster through liquids and solids than it does through gases. For example, sound travels more than four times faster through water than it does through air.

LOOK UP: Atoms and Molecules, Hearing, Light and Color, Motion, Radio

Space Flight

SPACE FLIGHT BEGAN WHEN ROCKETS BECAME POWERFUL ENOUGH TO LAUNCH SATELLITES INTO ORBIT.

SPUTNIK

On October 4, 1957, the Soviet Union launched the first artificial satellite into orbit. This satellite, called Sputnik 1, was a small steel sphere with four antennae. It contained nothing more than a radio transmitter and batteries.

A few weeks later, the Soviet Union launched a much larger satellite, Sputnik 2, which carried some scientific instruments and a dog named Laika. Although Laika died a week later when the oxygen inside Sputnik 2 ran out, her survival for that week proved that living things could survive both a rocket launch and the "weightless" conditions in space.

HUMANS IN SPACE

On April 12, 1961, Soviet cosmonaut Yuri Gagarin became the first human in space. His Vostok 1 mission lasted 108 minutes and included a single orbit of Earth before reentry. Project Mercury astronaut Alan Shepard became the first American in space when he made a fifteen-minute flight on May 5, 1961. On February 20, 1962, nearly a year after Gagarin's flight, John Glenn became the first American to orbit the planet. During his five-hour flight, Glenn ate a snack especially designed for space travel. It was packed in a tube like toothpaste.

APOLLO PROGRAM

In 1961, soon after the Soviets beat the Americans into orbit, President John F. Kennedy committed the

Sputnik 1

1 • EACH APOLLO MISSION began with the launch of a Saturn V rocket. The rocket's first two stages boosted the three astronauts into Earth orbit before dropping away. After a single orbit, the third stage was fired, sending the spacecraft toward the Moon.

1

4

4 • UPON RETURNING TO EARTH, the command module separated from the service module before its reentry and splashdown in the ocean.

United States to "landing a man on the Moon and returning him safely to Earth" before the end of the decade.

In December 1968, the crew of Apollo 8 became the first humans to orbit the Moon. On July 20, 1969, Apollo 11 astronauts Neil Armstrong and Edwin "Buzz" Aldrin, Jr., landed safely on the Moon, planting a flag and collecting some rock samples. Armstrong and Aldrin landed on the Moon's surface in the lunar excursion module *Eagle*, while fellow astronaut Michael Collins remained in orbit aboard the command module *Columbia*.

MIR

The most ambitious space station yet developed is the Soviet station Mir, which was launched in February 1986. Its design allows additional modules, such as laboratories and living quarters, to be added on as needed.

Today, Mir houses up to six cosmonauts, whose spacecraft can dock at any one of six ports. Cosmonauts live aboard Mir for a year or more before returning to Earth.

2 • DURING THE THREE-DAY TRIP TO THE MOON, the command module (with the crew inside) separated from the third stage, which also fell away. Still joined to the service module, the command module turned around and docked with the lunar module.

2

3

ASTRONAUTS train for the weightless conditions of space in large swimming pools and on specially equipped airplanes.

3 • AFTER REACHING THE MOON, the lunar module separated from the command module and landed on the surface. After completing their tasks, the astronauts took off again, regained orbit, and docked with the command module for the return trip to Earth.

Space Shuttle

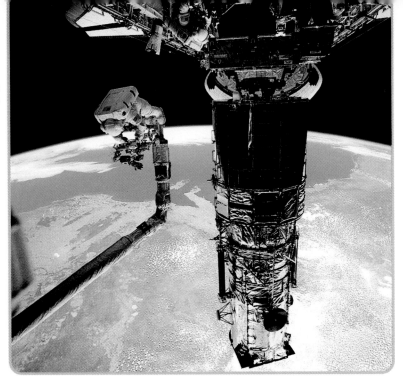

External tank

Orbiter

Solid rocket boosters

THE SPACE SHUTTLE IS A REUSABLE SPACECRAFT THAT TAKES OFF LIKE A ROCKET, FLIES LIKE A SPACESHIP, AND LANDS ON A RUNWAY LIKE AN AIRPLANE.

THE SPACE SHUTTLE was developed so that astronauts could travel back and forth into space on a regular basis. Its first mission was flown in 1981.

PARTS

The three main parts of the space shuttle are the solid rocket boosters, the external tank, and the orbiter.

The job of the solid rocket boosters is to lift the shuttle off the launchpad. Once their solid fuel is used up, they fall away from the shuttle.

Parachutes carry them safely back to Earth.

The external tank holds the liquid fuel that powers the shuttle's main engines. Eight and a half minutes after liftoff, the main engines shut off and the external tank falls away, burning up in the atmosphere. It is the only component of the shuttle that is not reusable.

The orbiter contains the crew compartment and the payload bay, which holds the shuttle's cargo. The top level of the crew compartment is the flight deck, where the pilots control the shuttle's

engines. The next level is the mid deck, where the crew works, sleeps, and relaxes. The bottom level is the equipment bay.

USES

The space shuttle is used to launch new satellites as well as retrieve and repair broken ones. It is also used as a laboratory for experiments in space.

Most shuttle crews have eight astronauts. Their missions usually last seven to ten days.

 LOOK UP: Flight, Rockets, Satellites, Space Flight

Spiders

It takes a SPIDER about an hour to spin a web. The spider begins by attaching its thread to a supporting structure, such as a window frame or the branches of a tree. Once the supporting threads are in place, the spider weaves the central spiral from the inside out.

SPIDERS ARE SMALL ANIMALS THAT EAT INSECTS. MANY SPIN WEBS TO TRAP THEIR PREY.

◀▷▲▽◀◀▷▲▽▷◀▽

LIKE INSECTS, SPIDERS are invertebrates, which means they have no backbone. Instead, they have a hard outer skeleton that they shed as they grow.

Spiders are often mistakenly grouped with insects, but there are important differences between them. Insects have six legs, while spiders have eight. Also, spiders have two body segments instead of three, and they lack the antennae, wings, and compound eyes that insects have.

Scientists separate insects and spiders into different taxonomic groups. Insects are placed in the class Insecta, while spiders belong to the class Arachnida. Other arachnids include scorpions, ticks, and mites.

◀▷▲▽◀◀▷▲▷◀▽

SPIDER WEBS

Spiders use spinnerets to spin their webs. These tiny nozzles, located in the spider's abdomen, are fed by glands that produce liquid silk. The spinnerets release thin streams of liquid silk that turn into sticky threads as they meet the air.

Many spiders wait in the center of their webs for the vibrations that mean food has landed. After capturing an insect, a spider uses its fangs to inject digestive juices into the insect's shell. These juices dissolve the guts of the insect, which the spider then sucks out.

Not all spiders spin webs. Some use their silk to lasso insects, while others drop a net of silk over their prey.

LOOK UP: Animals, Biology, Insects

Stars

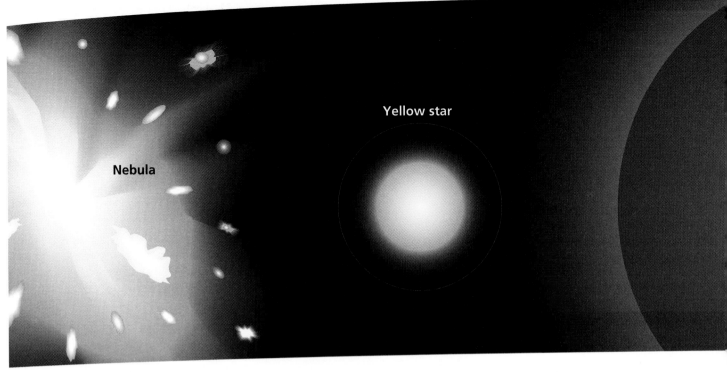

Nebula

Yellow star

STARS ARE GLOWING BALLS OF GAS, MADE UP MOSTLY OF HYDROGEN AND HELIUM.

NEW STARS ARE constantly forming. They form when clouds of gas and cosmic dust, called nebulae, collapse in on themselves.

FORMATION

As a nebula collapses, the hydrogen atoms inside it are packed tighter and tighter together. The collisions of these atoms inside the cloud's core make the temperature rise.

When the temperature reaches about eighteen million degrees Fahrenheit, the hydrogen atoms in the nebula's core join together to form helium atoms.

This process, called nuclear fusion, produces huge amounts of energy. This energy slowly makes its way to the star's surface, where it is released into space as radiation.

MAGNITUDE

Stars have different brightnesses, or magnitudes. A star's brightness as seen from Earth is called its apparent magnitude.

The brightest star in Earth's sky is Sirius, which is 8.6 light years away. Other stars shine more brightly than Sirius, but they seem dimmer to people on Earth because they are much farther away than Sirius.

LIFESPAN

Just as stars form, they also die. The Sun is now about halfway through its expected lifespan of ten billion years. Five billion years from now, when all its hydrogen has been converted into helium, the yellow Sun will swell into a huge red ball called a red giant.

After a few million years, the thin outer layers of the red giant will blow away, leaving a shrunken core called a white dwarf. The Sun will then slowly fade until it goes out entirely, becoming a black dwarf.

Stars up to five times the mass of the Sun become red giants and then white dwarves. But stars that are much larger than the Sun lead very different lives. They burn much hotter and faster,

Red giant

White dwarf

Black dwarf

living only ten million years. Then they die in massive explosions called supernovas.

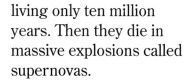

BLACK HOLES

When a very large star explodes in a supernova, it leaves behind a "corpse" that can form a black hole. Black holes form when the mass of a dead star is so great that gravity pulls its remains closer and closer together.

The dead star shrinks so much that the force of its gravity becomes too strong for anything, even light, to escape it.

Because light can never leave a black hole, it is impossible to see one. Astronomers can detect black holes only by the effect their gravity has on nearby stars.

When the Sun becomes a red giant, it will swell to one hundred times its present size, swallowing Mercury and Venus and filling up half the sky as seen from Earth.

Sun

THE SUN IS THE STAR AROUND WHICH EARTH ORBITS. THE AVERAGE DISTANCE BETWEEN THE SUN AND EARTH IS NINETY-THREE MILLION MILES.

THE SUN IS 4.6 BILLION years old, the same age as the planets. It contains ninety-nine percent of the mass of the solar system. Its size, life span, and brightness are all average for a star.

Patches called SUNSPOTS sometimes appear in groups on the Sun's surface. They are areas of cooler gas, where magnetic storms have interrupted the flow of heat from the Sun's core.

The Sun's huge mass provides the gravity that holds the solar system together. The Sun's gravity keeps the planets, asteroids, and comets in their proper orbits.

SIZE AND TEMPERATURE

At its widest point, the diameter of the Sun, or the distance through it, is 865,000 miles. More than one million Earths could fit inside the Sun, which rotates completely once every 25.4 Earth days.

The Sun's surface temperature is about ten thousand degrees Fahrenheit. The temperature at its core is much hotter, being closer to twenty-seven million degrees Fahrenheit. In comparison, lead melts and turns to gas at just three thousand degrees Fahrenheit.

The arches and loops of flaming gas on the Sun's surface are called prominences. Sometimes these prominences explode, creating bursts of super-hot gas called solar flares.

On the Sun's surface, gas bubbles swirl around, creating a speckled texture.

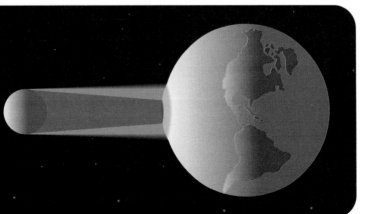

SOLAR ECLIPSE • When the Moon moves between Earth and the Sun, a solar eclipse occurs. During a solar eclipse, the Moon blocks some of the Sun's light from reaching Earth. In some places on Earth, the Sun appears at times to be completely hidden. This is called a full eclipse. In other places, only part of the Sun is blocked. This is a partial eclipse.

LOOK UP: Astronomy, Gravity, Planets, Solar System, Stars

Taste

Your senses of taste and smell work together. When you eat, you taste and smell your food at the same time. When you have a cold and your nose is clogged, your food will have less taste than it usually does.

TASTE IS THE SENSE PROVIDED BY YOUR TONGUE AND MOUTH.

YOUR SENSE OF TASTE is closely linked to your sense of smell. Both detect chemicals.

Your nose detects odors, or chemicals in the air. Your tongue and mouth detect tastes, which are chemicals in your food.

TASTE BUDS

Both your mouth and your tongue contain taste buds. These are groups of receptor cells that sense chemicals in your food.

As you chew, chemicals from the food dissolve in your saliva. Your saliva carries those chemicals to your taste buds.

Inside your taste buds are nerve cells. When these nerve cells are stimulated by chemicals, they produce electrical messages, which are sent to your brain. These messages tell your brain what you are eating.

FLAVOR

Different taste buds sense different tastes. Some of your taste buds respond to sweet flavors. Some detect salty flavors. There are also taste buds that detect sour flavors, and there are still others that pick up bitter flavors.

The complicated tastes produced by most foods are combinations of these four flavors.

The bumps on your tongue are TASTE BUDS.

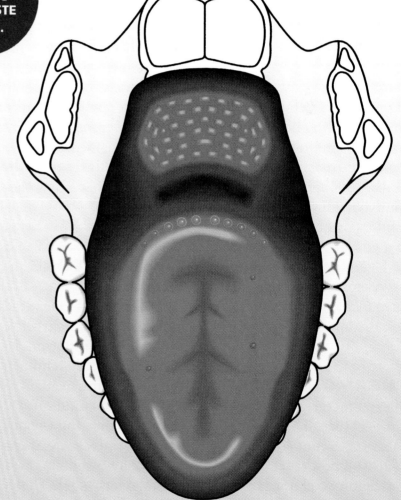

Temperature

TEMPERATURE IS A MEASURE OF HOW HOT AN OBJECT IS.

HEAT IS A FORM OF energy. Adding heat to a substance makes its molecules move faster. Adding enough heat can change a substance from a solid to a liquid or a liquid to a gas.

Even the coldest objects have some heat. They just have less heat than warmer objects do.

THERMOMETERS

Thermometers measure temperature. They use substances that conduct heat well and react noticeably to changes in temperature. Mercury, for example, expands a lot as it gets hotter.

The most common thermometers are glass tubes filled with mercury. As heat increases, the mercury inside the tube expands. Markings on the side of the tube show the temperature.

TEMPERATURE SCALES

Temperature is measured in degrees. But degrees can stand for different temperatures depending on the scale being used.

Scientists (and most countries) use the Celsius, or centigrade, scale, devised in 1742 by Swedish astronomer Anders Celsius. He made 0°C the boiling point of water and 100°C its freezing point. Other scientists soon reversed these numbers.

People in the United States use the Fahrenheit scale. According to this scale, water freezes at 32°F and boils at 212°F. Each degree centigrade equals almost two degrees Fahrenheit.

The lowest temperature imaginable is ABSOLUTE ZERO. Theoretically, all molecules would stop moving at this temperature. Scientists have created conditions within 0.00001°C of absolute zero, but they believe they can never reach it completely.

Fahrenheit	Centigrade
Inside a star 27,000,000°F	5,000,000°C
Inside a volcano 2,700°F	1,500°C
Water boils 212°F	110°C
Normal body temperature 98.6°F	37°C
Water freezes 32°F	0°C
Mercury freezes -38°F	-39°C
Oxygen freezes -361°F	-218°C
Absolute zero -460°F	-273°C

LOOK UP: *Energy, Matter, Measurement, Scientific Method*

Touch

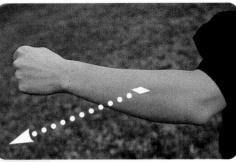

TOUCH IS THE SENSE PROVIDED BY YOUR SKIN.

SKIN IS THE LAYER of tissue that covers the outside of your body. One of its purposes is to protect the delicate tissue inside your body.

Skin also keeps your body from becoming too hot or too cold, and it prevents harmful bacteria from entering your body.

LAYERS

The top layer of your skin is called the epidermis. Skin cells at the bottom of the epidermis are constantly dividing. These new cells replace dead skin cells on the surface as they wear and flake away.

The dermis is a thicker layer of skin cells beneath the epidermis. It contains blood vessels, glands, hair roots, and nerve endings.

Capillaries feed the skin cells and take waste away.

They also help regulate your temperature. When you get too hot—during exercise, for example—your blood circulates near the surface of your skin and releases heat into the air.

GLANDS

Sweat glands also help control your body's temperature. They produce sweat, which evaporates to cool your body.

Oil glands in the dermis produce a substance called sebum. Sebum lubricates your skin.

RECEPTORS

Your skin also contains nerve endings called receptors. These receptors can sense heat and pressure.

Sensory nerves carry messages from the receptors in your skin to your brain. Your brain interprets these messages as touch.

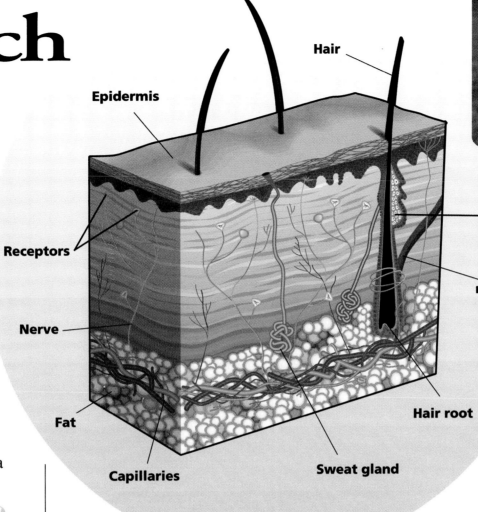

Hair

Epidermis

Receptors

Nerve

Fat

Capillaries

Oil gland

Hair muscle

Hair root

Sweat gland

LOOK UP: Brain, Human Body, Senses

Trees

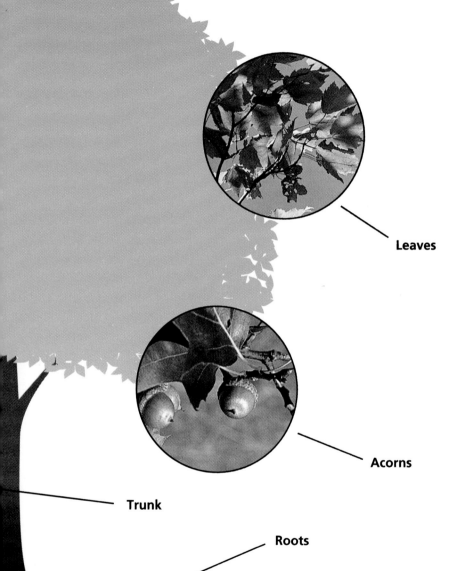

Leaves

Acorns

Trunk

Roots

TREES ARE LARGE PLANTS WITH A SINGLE WOODY STEM. ALL TREES BEAR FRUIT THAT PROTECT THEIR SEEDS.

MOST TREES ARE TALL. The tallest tree is the sequoia, which can grow more than three hundred feet tall. Trees can also be short. The snow willow, for example, is only one inch tall.

TYPES

There are two basic types of trees: the broadleaf and the conifer. Broad-leafed trees include oaks and maples. They are also called deciduous trees, which means they lose their leaves in the fall. Some deciduous trees have fruits, such as peaches and apples, that are pulpy and edible.

Coniferous trees include pines and spruces. They are commonly called evergreens because most of them remain green all year. Conifers get their name from cones, the kind of fruit they bear.

PARTS

Conifers and broad-leafed trees may look different, but most of their parts function in the same way. They both have roots that absorb water and nutrients from the soil. They also have trunks that carry the water and nutrients from the roots to the branches. Bark protects the trunk and the branches from animals and the weather.

The branches hold the leaves apart, so that each leaf can get as much sunlight as possible. Branches also support the fruit, which holds and protects the tree's seeds.

The compact shape and narrow leaves of conifers help

them survive even in cold climates. Because their needlelike leaves are small, they do not lose a lot of moisture to the wind. The angle of their branches also forces heavy snow to slide off conifers.

You can tell the age of this tree by counting its RINGS.

TREE RINGS

As trees grow, their trunks become thicker. For each year, trunks add a ring. You can tell the age of a tree by counting the number of rings in its trunk.

The world's oldest living trees are North American bristlecone pines. Some of these trees, which grow in the Rocky Mountains, are nearly five thousand years old.

HABITAT

Various species of birds, monkeys, reptiles, and insects make their homes in trees. Some animals, such as the South American opossum, never go down to the forest floor. Others, such as worms and badgers, burrow beneath trees to make their homes among the thick roots.

Trees are important to the environment. Like all plants, they give off oxygen that people and other animals need to breathe. Their leaves also help shade and cool the earth's surface from the hot rays of the sun. Many sensitive plants would die without some shade.

The needle-shaped LEAVES of a conifer have the same function as the larger, flatter leaves of a broadleaf. That is, they use sunlight to produce food for the tree. This process is called photosynthesis.

CONES are the fruit of the pine tree. Like nuts, berries, and acorns, they protect the seeds of the tree.

LOOK UP: Climate, Ecology, Flowers, Forest, Fruits and Seeds, Plants, Soil

Universe

THE UNIVERSE INCLUDES ALL THE MATTER THAT EXISTS AND ALL THE SPACE IT OCCUPIES.

UNTIL THE 1600S, NEARLY everyone believed that Earth was the center of the universe. People thought the stars were lights painted on a huge sphere surrounding the planet.

Earth is one of nine known planets in our solar system, which is part of a galaxy called the Milky Way in a cluster of about thirty galaxies called the Local Group. Clusters are the largest structures in the universe. Each cluster may contain a few dozen galaxies or many thousands.

SIZE

Since then, astronomers have shown that Earth is just one tiny dot in a universe too big for most people to imagine.

Astronomers estimate that there are one hundred billion galaxies in the vast universe. They estimate that each galaxy itself contains an average of one hundred billion stars.

BIG BANG

Scientists have a number of theories about how the universe began. The most widely accepted is the big bang theory.

According to the big bang theory, the universe formed in a huge explosion between eight and fifteen billion years ago. As time passed, the pull of gravity brought atoms together to form galaxies, stars, and planets.

EXPANDING UNIVERSE

Earlier in this century, astronomers discovered that the galaxies in the universe are moving away from one another. In other words, the universe is expanding.

Some astronomers believe that the universe will keep expanding forever. Others think a time will come billions of years from now when the universe will stop expanding and collapse again in a big crunch.

10,000,000,000,000,000,000,000,000

Scientists estimate that there are this many stars in the universe.

LOOK UP: Astronomy, Galaxies, Gravity, Planets, Solar System, Stars

Volcanoes

VOLCANOES ARE VENTS IN THE EARTH'S CRUST FROM WHICH MOLTEN ROCK, ASH, AND STEAM FLOW.

SOME VOLCANOES erupt regularly, releasing molten rock, or magma, in steady streams. These volcanoes often form over hot spots where magma from the earth's mantle rises up through the crust in long cracks, or fissures. Most fissure volcanoes occur along deep trenches under the ocean, where they help build tectonic plates.

Conical volcanoes are found on land and along plate margins. Unlike fissure volcanoes, conical volcanoes tend to erupt violently. They often send huge clouds of ash and steam high into the atmosphere.

ERUPTIONS

Conical volcanoes typically have steep sides and craters at their peaks. At their roots are reservoirs of molten rock called magma chambers.

Funnel-shaped vents carry steam to the surface. When these vents become blocked with debris from previous eruptions, pressure builds up in the magma chamber. When enough pressure builds up, the volcano erupts with explosive force.

LAVA

Lava is the name given to magma that reaches the surface. As lava flows down the sides of a volcano, it cools and forms igneous rocks such as basalt and obsidian.

The eruption of an undersea volcano can sometimes form a volcanic island. The island of Surtsey was formed when a volcano off the coast of Iceland erupted in 1963.

Volcanoes often form along the edges of tectonic plates when one plate is pushed down by the other. The leading edge of the plate that is pushed down melts to form magma. This magma accumulates until enough pressure builds up for an eruption.

Crater

Lava

Vent

Magma chamber

Weather

In a **LOW-PRESSURE SYSTEM**, air rises. Because air cools as it rises, moisture in the air condenses to form clouds. Low-pressure systems often produce stormy weather.

In a **HIGH-PRESSURE SYSTEM**, air sinks to the ground, where its gas molecules are squeezed closer together, warming them. The result is warm, dry, and clear weather.

WEATHER REFERS TO CHANGING CONDITIONS IN THE EARTH'S ATMOSPHERE.

FOUR CONDITIONS OF the air—temperature, movement, pressure, and humidity—have the most effect on weather. They interact in different ways to create different weather patterns.

TEMPERATURE

Differences in air temperature are the most important causes of weather. As the sun heats the earth's surface, the earth in turn heats the air directly above it.

But the sun does not heat all regions of the earth equally. The region around the equator, for example, has warmer air than either of the polar regions.

MOVEMENT

These differences in air temperature create pressure differences that cause the air movement we call wind. As warm air above the equator rises, cool air from the polar regions moves in to replace it.

This movement carries warm air to cooler regions. Wind also carries air from areas of high pressure to areas of low pressure.

PRESSURE

Air pressure is the degree to which the gas molecules in air are squeezed together by the weight of atmosphere above them. It can vary depending on the temperature of the air in a particular region.

When air is warmed by the sun, it rises, creating an area of low pressure beneath it. Similarly, sinking cold air creates an area of high pressure.

HUMIDITY

All air contains some moisture, or water that has evaporated. The amount of moisture in air is called its humidity.

The moist air above a rain forest has a high humidity. The dry air over a desert has a low humidity.

AIR MASSES

Air masses are bodies of air with the same temperature, pressure, and humidity. Air masses that form at sea pick up water from the ocean, which makes them moist. Those that form over deserts are hot and dry.

Moving air masses bring changes in the weather. For example, when warm, humid air moves into a cool region, the moisture in it condenses and falls to the ground as rain or snow.

METEOROLOGY

Meteorology is the study of weather. Meteorologists use instruments, such as thermometers and barometers that measure air masses. They use the information they collect to predict the weather.

Meteorologists keep some of these instruments at weather stations on land and others on weather ships at sea. They also use weather satellites orbiting in space to gather data about the earth's weather patterns.

Meteorologists use **WEATHER MAPS** to show the locations of fronts. A front is the boundary between two different air masses. It usually takes about a day for a front to move through an area. Whenever that happens, the weather changes.

▲ Blue triangles show the leading edge of a cold front, or mass of cold air.

◗ Red semicircles show the leading edge of a warm front, or mass of warm air.

H The letter H indicates a high-pressure system

L The letter L indicates a low-pressure system.

Wind

WIND IS THE MOVEMENT OF AIR IN THE ATMOSPHERE.

TROPICAL AIR AT THE equator is warmer than the polar air around it. This temperature difference is an important cause of the world's winds.

As warm air at the equator rises and spreads, it forms a low-pressure area. Cool air from the poles moves in to replace it. This movement of air is wind.

Wind blows from high-pressure weather systems to low-pressure ones. The bigger the pressure difference, the stronger the wind.

WIND TURBINES use the force of the wind to generate electricity. They do not pollute the air or water, but they are noisy and take up a large amount of land.

Polar easterlies

Westerlies

Trade winds

Trade winds

Westerlies

Polar easterlies

JET STREAMS are powerful currents of air that move about six miles above the earth's surface. They circle the globe even faster than the prevailing winds. Jet streams can be two miles deep and hundreds of miles wide. They change position depending on temperature differences between the poles and the equator. They can move north and south as well as up and down. There are four major jet streams, two in each hemisphere. They all blow from west to east at about 35 miles per hour in the summer and 90 miles per hour in the winter. However, wind speeds up to 310 miles per hour have been recorded in jet streams. Eastbound airplane pilots often travel in jet streams to cut their flight times.

PREVAILING WINDS

Winds that blow in constant, predictable patterns are called prevailing winds. Among the world's prevailing winds are the westerlies, the polar easterlies, and the trade winds.

Because of the earth's rotation, the prevailing winds move in circular patterns. This is called the Coriolis effect.

BEAUFORT SCALE

Wind strength can be measured using the Beaufort scale. The Beaufort scale ranges from zero, which means no wind, to twelve, which means hurricane-force winds.

At zero on the Beaufort scale, smoke rises straight up. With force-four winds, small trees sway and ripples form on lakes. A force-nine gale moving at fifty miles per hour can blow the shingles off a roof.

Glossary

acid rain • Acid rain is a form of pollution. Coal-burning factories produce sulfur dioxide gas, which combines with water in the air to form acid rain.

altitude • Altitude measures the height above the earth's surface of an object such as a mountain or an airplane.

arithmetic • Arithmetic is the branch of mathematics whose operations include addition, subtraction, multiplication, and division.

asteroid • An asteroid is a piece of rock that travels around the sun like a small planet.

atom • An atom is the smallest piece of an element. Its parts include protons, neutrons, and electrons.

big bang theory • According to the big bang theory, the universe was formed in a huge explosion that happened between eight and fifteen billion years ago.

botany • Botany is the study of plants.

capillary • Capillaries are the smallest blood vessels.

carnivore • A carnivore is a living thing that eats meat.

cell • Cells are the smallest parts of most living things. The human body is made up of trillions of different cells, such as nerve cells and muscle cells, that work together.

celestial • The word *celestial* describes objects in the sky such as the moon, the planets, and the stars.

chemistry • Chemistry is the study of the elements and the compounds they make.

circuit • A circuit is a loop of conductive material through which electricity flows.

circumference • The circumference of an object is the distance around it.

cold-blooded • Cold-blooded animals, such as reptiles, have body temperatures that change with the temperature of the surrounding air.

compound • A compound is a substance made up of two or more elements that have joined together. Water is a compound of hydrogen and oxygen.

condensation • Condensation is the process by which a gas changes into a liquid.

conductor • A conductor is a substance, such as metallic wire, through which electricity travels.

conifer • A conifer is an evergreen tree, such as a pine or a spruce, that bears cones as its fruit.

cosmonaut • *Cosmonaut* is the Russian term for *astronaut*.

crust • The crust is the surface layer of the earth. It is made up of rocks and soil.

current • Current is the flow of electricity through a circuit. It is also a river-like band of warm or cool water that flows through the ocean.

data • Data is unorganized information collected by scientists as the result of observation and experimentation.

deciduous tree • Deciduous trees, such as oaks and maples, lose their leaves in the fall.

diameter • The diameter of a circle or a sphere is the distance across it at its widest point.

ecosystem • An ecosystem is a community made up of living things and the nonliving things that affect them. Deserts and lakes are examples of ecosystems.

electricity • Electricity is a form of energy made up of electrons moving in a stream.

electron • An electron is one of the parts of an atom. It moves around the nucleus at nearly the speed of light.

electronics • Electronics is the technology that controls electrical currents. Electronic machines include computers and digital watches.

element • An element is a pure substance.

energy • Energy can change the state and position of matter. Heat, light, and sound are all forms of energy.

environment • An environment is the combination of nonliving things, such as the soil and the climate, that affect the living things in an ecosystem.

equator • The equator is an imaginary line around the middle of the earth halfway between the North and South poles.

erosion • Erosion is the wearing away of rocks and soil by wind and water.

evaporation • Evaporation is the process by which a liquid changes into a gas.

evolution • Evolution is the process by which living things change and develop over time.

extinction • The word *extinction* means the dying out of a species of living thing. A species is considered extinct when it has not been seen in the wild for fifty years.

force • Force is a push or pull. It transfers energy from one object to another.

fossil • A fossil is the remains of an ancient living thing that has been preserved in rock.

friction • Friction is a form of heat energy. It is produced when two objects, such as a brake and a bicycle wheel, rub against each other.

function • The function of an object or activity is its purpose or use.

galaxy • A galaxy is a collection of stars and other celestial objects. The Milky Way is the galaxy in which we live.

genetics • Genetics is the study of how characteristics are passed on from one generation of living things to another.

geology • Geology is the study of the earth's composition and its history as a planet.

gravity • Gravity is a force of attraction between two objects. The earth's gravity pulls objects toward it.

habitat • Habitats are places where plants and animals live. In forests, for example, trees are the most common habitat.

herbivore • An herbivore is a living thing that eats plants.

humidity • Humidity measures the amount of moisture in the air.

invertebrate • Invertebrates are animals that do not have a backbone. Insects, worms, and shellfish are all examples of invertebrates.

kinetic energy • Kinetic energy is the energy of a moving object, such as a bowling ball or a rocket.

larva • A larva is an insect at an early stage in its life cycle. A larva may also be called a caterpillar.

light year • A light year is the distance a ray of light travels in one year. Light years are nearly six trillion miles long.

magma • Magma is hot, liquid rock found deep underground. Magma that reaches the surface is called lava.

magnification • The magnification of a microscope or telescope measures the degree to which it can enlarge objects for viewing.

mantle • The mantle is the layer of the earth between the crust and the core.

mass • Mass measures the amount of matter in an object. It is the same in space and on the earth.

matter • Matter is anything that takes up space and has weight.

metabolism • Metabolism is the process by which the cells of a living thing turn food into energy.

meteorology • Meteorology is the study of the weather.

molecule • A molecule is made up of two or more atoms that have joined together.

molten • A molten substance, such as molten rock, is a normally solid material that has been turned into a liquid by heat.

neutron • A neutron is one of the parts of an atom. Neutrons, along with protons, make up the nucleus of an atom.

niche • A niche is a place in an ecosystem where a species of living thing finds food and shelter.

nucleus • The nucleus of an atom is its center. It is a cluster of protons and neutrons around which electrons spin. The nucleus of a cell controls the cell's activities and stores its genetic information.

nutrient • Nutrients are the basic units of food that cells use for energy.

omnivore • An omnivore is a living thing that eats both plants and meat.

orbit • An orbit is the path that one celestial object, such as a satellite or a planet, takes around another.

organ • Organs are body parts, such as the heart or the brain, that perform specific functions.

organism • An organism is a living thing. Plants, animals, fungi, protists, and monerans are all organisms.

paleontology • Paleontology is the study of prehistoric life. Paleontologists study fossils to learn more about life during earlier geological periods.

photosynthesis • Photosynthesis is the chemical process by which plants turn water and carbon dioxide into food and oxygen.

plate margins • Plate margins are the edges of the tectonic plates that make up the earth's crust. Most volcanoes and mountains form along plate margins.

pollution • Pollution is the release of waste into the environment. It is often ugly and can also be dangerous.

potential energy • Energy that is stored is called potential energy. Fuels, such as gasoline, are high in potential energy.

precipitation • Precipitation is water that falls from clouds. Rain and snow are forms of precipitation.

predator • Predators are animals that hunt other animals for food.

prey • Animals hunted by other animals for food are called prey.

proton • A proton is one of the parts of an atom. Protons, along with neutrons, make up the nucleus of an atom.

radiation • Radiation is a form of energy given off as waves or particles. Light, sound, and radioactivity are examples of radiation.

radioactivity • Radioactivity is the process by which certain atoms give off energy as they split apart.

reproduction • Reproduction is the process by which living things create new life.

satellite • A satellite is a natural or articifical object that orbits a large celestial body such as a planet.

sea level • Sea level is the level of the surface of the sea from which the height of a mountain or the depth of an ocean is measured.

sediment • Sediment consists of rock particles that collect on river and ocean bottoms.

solar eclipse • A solar eclipse occurs when the moon moves between the sun and the earth, stopping some of the sun's rays from reaching the earth.

solar energy • Solar energy is energy that comes from the sun in the form of light and heat.

spawn • Spawn are eggs laid in the water by fish and amphibians.

species • A species is a group of living things that have common characteristics. The grizzly, for example, is a species of bear, and the lily is a species of flower.

substance • A substance is anything that has weight and takes up space. Substances are also called matter.

suburb • A suburb is a small community near a city.

symbiosis • Symbiosis is the relationship of two living things working together for the benefit of both.

taxonomy • Taxonomy is the system that scientists use to classify living things into categories.

tectonic plate • Tectonic plates are huge masses of rock on which the continents and the oceans rest.

transmit • To transmit is to send from one person, place, or thing to another.

ultraviolet rays • Ultraviolet rays are invisible light waves that are found in sunlight and other sources.

vertebrate • Vertebrates are animals that have a backbone. Birds, fish, and mammals are examples of vertebrates.

warm-blooded • Warm-blooded animals, such as birds and mammals, have body temperatures that remain about the same in hot and cold weather.

weight • Weight depends both on mass and on the pull of gravity. An object's weight decreases as the pull of gravity weakens.

Index

solid state of matter, 44, 109

sonograms, 139

sound, 60, 85, 98, 101, 126, 139, 149, 158-159

space flight, 21, 144, 156-157, 160-162

space shuttle, 162

space station, 161

sparrows, 25

spawn, 17, 97

sperm whales, 125

spiders, 150, 163

spinal cord, 30

spinetail swifts, 19

spinnerets, 163

spores, 129

spring lobsters, 151

Sputnik 1, 160

Sputnik 2, 160

squamates, 140

squid, 151

squirrels, 54-55, 71, 87

stamen, 68

stars, 75, 127, 132, 164-166, 172

static electricity, 57

steel, 111

stigma, 68

stomach, 48-49

stratosphere, 22

stratus clouds, 35

subatomic particles, 23

submarines, 45

subsoil, 155

Sun, 60, 75, 121, 127, 148, 156, 164-166

sunspots, 21, 166

superconductors, 57

supernovas, 165

surface gravity, 115

surgeonfish, 42

Surtsey, 173

swallows, 114

swans, 29

sweat glands, 169

symbiosis, 42, 125

T

tadpoles, 17

tapeworms, 125

taste, 149, 167

taste buds, 167

taxonomy, 26-27, 163

tectonic plates, 40-41, 53, 117, 173

teeth, 48

telescopes, 20-21, 149, 157

temperature, 168

tendons, 118, 153

termites, 83

Tertiary period, 79

tetanus, 113

thermodynamics, 126

thermometers, 168, 175

thermosphere, 22

Thomson's gazelles, 82

three-toed sloths, 137

thrust, 67

thunderstorms, 57, 91, 135

ticks, 125, 163

tides, 84, 121

tigers, 31

toads, 16, 31

tongue, 167

topsoil, 155

tornadoes, 90-91

tortoises, 18, 140

toucans, 137

touch, 149, 154, 169

trace fossils, 72

trachea, 100-101

trade winds, 176

tree rings, 171

trees, 70, 170-171

Triassic period, 79

tributaries, 143

triceps, 118

Triceratops, 50

trilobites, 73

troposphere, 22, 35

tuataras, 141

turtles, 114, 140

typhoons, 91

typhus, 125

Tyrannosaurus rex, 50

U

ultraviolet radiation, 22, 124

universe, 75, 172

Uranus, 21, 156-157

uterus, 107, 138-139

V

variables, 108
vegetables, 74, 129
veins, 86, 88
velocity, 116
Venus, 21, 127, 156, 165
vertebrates, 16, 18, 28, 64, 140
vibration, 116
Viking 1, 156
villi, 49
visible spectrum, 99, 135
vitamins, 119
vocal cords, 101
voice box, 101
volcanoes, 40, 120, 145, 173
volts, 56-57
voluntary actions, 30
Vostok 1, 160
Voyager space probes, 21, 157
vultures, 82

W

water cycle, 134-135
water lilies, 95
watersheds, 142
waterspouts, 91
waves, ocean, 121
weather, 22, 34-35, 77, 90-91, 115, 146,
        148, 174-176
webs, 163
weight, 67, 84, 109-110, 126
westerlies, 176

wetlands, 94
whale sharks, 64
whales, 107, 114
wheels, 102-103
whelks, 150
white dwarf stars, 164-165
white-tailed deer, 25
wildebeests, 82-83
wind, 14-15, 90-91, 121, 145, 174, 176
wind energy, 61, 176
wind tunnels, 15
wind turbines, 61, 176
windmills, 61
windpipe, 100-101
wolverines, 71
wolves, 107
womb, 107, 139
woodpeckers, 70
worms, 18, 171

X

X rays, 98

Y

yeast, 113
Yosemite Valley, 81

Z

zebras, 82
zoology, 26
zooplankton, 42
zooxanthellae, 42

Photo & Illustration Credits

COVER—All images Breck P. Kent, except for: Moon, nebula, Saturn, space shuttle (National Aeronautics and Space Adminstration); beakers, prism, microscope (Nasco); kids (David Waitz); train (French Government Tourist Office); scuba diver (Tim Molloy).

ELMO—Model: Emma Vignola
Photographer: Tilman Reitzle

INTERIOR—**Peter Arnold:** 12, 33, 65 (top), 104 (top right), 105 (top right), 112 (top right, bottom), 113 (bottom right), 116 (top), 125 (right), 134 (bottom), 147 (top), 158 (top); **Raymond Smith:** 13 (top), 36 (top right), 51, 78, 79 (bottom left, bottom right); **Breck P. Kent:** 13 (bottom left, bottom right), 15 (left), 16, 17 (bottom left), 18 (bottom center, bottom right), 19 (bottom left), 29 (bottom left), 31 (bottom), 36 (top left), 44 (top right, bottom), 45 (bottom), 50 (right), 53 (top), 57 (top), 59 (top right), 60-61, 61, 63 (bottom), 64 (right), 66 (top), 72, 73 (top right, bottom), 76 (left), 81 (right), 85 (top right), 86 (top right), 87 (left), 93, 99 (bottom), 107 (top left, bottom right), 111 (top left), 113 (top), 123 (bottom), 128, 133, 135, 140 (top, bottom left), 145 (top, insets), 147 (bottom), 149 (top), 151 (bottom left), 154 (right), 171 (left), 176 (bottom); **Rita Lascaro:** 14 (left), 15 (bottom right), 23, 34, 40, 41 (top, center), 53 (bottom), 109, 110 (top right), 112 (top left), 114 (top left), 120 (top), 121, 168, 176 (top); **General Motors Corporation:** 15 (top right); **Alan Irikura:** 16-17, 18-19, 19 (top,

center), 26-27, 29 (top), 44 (top left), 52 (bottom), 63 (top right), 66 (bottom), 67, 68, 74, 75 (bottom), 77, 79 (center), 92 (top), 96, 96-97, 97 (center), 98-99, 99 (center), 104 (left, bottom right), 105 (bottom), 113 (bottom left), 115 (bottom), 122, 124, 126 (right), 127, 129, 130-131, 132, 145 (center), 146 (left), 148, 151 (bottom right), 155, 156-157, 157, 159 (right), 160-161, 164-165, 165, 166 (bottom left, bottom right), 170 (left), 170-171, 171 (right), 172, 175 (right); **Zoological Society of San Diego:** 17 (bottom right), 59 (bottom), 141 (top right, bottom); **Wildlife Collection:** 18 (bottom left/Jack Swenson), 19 (bottom right/D. Robert Franz), 28 (left/Martin Harvey, right/Charles Melton), 29 (bottom right/John Giustina), 31 (top/John Giustina), 50 (left/Michael Rothman), 63 (top left/Mauricio Handler, top center/Tim Laman), 64 (left/Chris Huss), 65 (bottom/Chris Huss), 87 (right/Michael Francis), 92 (bottom/Bob Parks), 97 (bottom/Chris Huss), 106 (Vivek Sinha), 107 (bottom left/Dean Lee, top right/Robert Lankinen), 114 (top right/Henry Holdsworth, bottom/Jo Overholt), 125 (left/Gary Bell), 140 (bottom right/Martin Harvey), 141 (top left/John Giustina), 150 (left/Chris Huss, right/Kenneth Deitcher), 151 (top/Chris Huss), 163 (Kenneth Deitcher); **NASA:** 20 (right), 21, 60 (left), 75 (top, center), 84 (left), 90, 115 (top), 126 (left), 144, 146 (right), 156, 159 (left), 160, 161, 162, 175 (left); **Slim Films:** 22 (Bryan Christie), 24-25 (Andy Christie), 30 (top/Bryan Christie, bottom/Pete Samek), 35 (Bryan Christie), 41 (bottom/Bryan Christie), 42-43 (Pete Samek), 46-47 (Pete Samek), 48-49 (Pete Samek), 52 (top/Pete Samek), 54-55 (Pete Samek), 62 (Bryan Christie), 69 (Bryan Christie), 70-71 (Pete Samek), 80 (Pete

Samek), 81 (left/Pete Samek), 82-83 (Pete Samek), 85 (bottom/Pete Samek), 86 (left/Pete Samek, bottom right/Pete Samek), 88-89 (Bryan Christie), 94-95 (Pete Samek), 100 (Pete Samek), 101 (left/Bryan Christie, center/Pete Samek), 102-103 (Pete Samek), 117 (Bryan Christie), 118 (Bryan Christie), 119 (Pete Samek), 134 (top/Bryan Christie), 136-137 (Pete Samek), 138 (Pete Samek), 139 (bottom/Bryan Christie), 142-143 (Pete Samek), 152 (Pete Samek), 153 (Pete Samek), 154 (left/Pete Samek), 167 (Pete Samek), 169 (left/Pete Samek), 173 (bottom/Bryan Christie), 174 (Bryan Christie); **United Mine Workers:** 36 (bottom); **Jet Proposion Laboratory:** 37 (top), 166 (top left); **Meteor Crater, Northern Arizona, U.S.A.:** 37 (bottom); **Apple Computers:** 38 (left); **Intel Corporation:** 38 (right), 58; **David Rubel:** 39 (right), 56, 57 (bottom), 98, 101 (right), 111 (top right), 116 (bottom), 123 (top), 169 (right), 170 (bottom right), 171 (top center); **U.S. Navy Office of Information:** 45 (top), 158 (bottom); **Thailand Tourist Office:** 55 (top); **Con Edison:** 60 (right); **Petrified Forest National Park:** 73 (top left); **Hewitt Rubel:** 76 (center), 108; **Joseph Glicksman:** 76 (right); **U.S. Geological Survey:** 79 (top); **Yosemite National Park:** 81 (right); **National Oceanic and Atmospheric Administration:** 91; **Nasco:** 105 (top left), 110 (bottom), 126 (top right); **Phelps Dodge Corporation:** 111 (bottom); **Woods Hole Oceanographic Institute:** 120 (bottom); **Jack Allen Jenkins:** 139 (top); **Clay Pit Ponds State Park Preserve, N.Y.:** 170 (top right), 171 (bottom center); **Iceland Tourist Board:** 173 (top).